Marcel Pagnol

L'Eau des collines:

Jean de Florette
Manon des sources

David Coward

Professor of Modern French Literature
University of Leeds.

UNIVERSITY OF GLASGOW
FRENCH AND GERMAN PUBLICATIONS
1993

University of Glasgow French and German Publications

Series Editors: Mark G. Ward (German)
                   Geoff Woollen (French)

Consultant Editors : Colin Smethurst
                     Kenneth Varty

Modern Languages Building, University of Glasgow,
Glasgow G12 8QL, Scotland.

First published 1990.
Revised and augmented edition published 1993.

Printed by BPCC Wheatons Ltd., Exeter.

ISBN 0 85261 391 1

Contents

Editions

Bracketed page number citations refer to the 1988 Fortunio texts published by Éditions de Fallois; where sense or chronology do not make it clear, or a sequence is broken, they are denoted by J for *Jean de Florette* and M for *Manon des sources*. Livre de Poche owners will be reassured to know that the page numbering of their volumes (to 318 for *Jean de Florette*; to 329 for *Manon des sources*) corresponds closely to Fortunio's 312 pages for each, and the necessary adjustments should therefore be easy to make. When reference is made to *La Gloire de mon père* (1957), *Le Château de ma mère* (1958) and *Le Temps des secrets* (1960), it is to the Éditions de Provence texts.

Pagnol Country

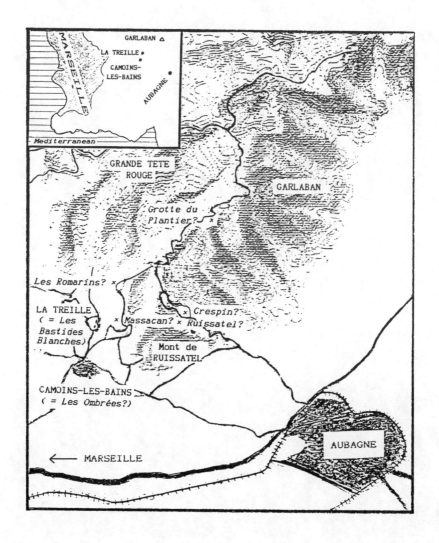

Chapter One

The Beginning: *Manon des sources* (1952)

In 1950, Marcel Pagnol (1895-1974) had still to reclaim the high position he had held in the 1930s when he was one of France's most successful and respected independent film makers. He had first made his name in the theatre in the twenties as an astringent social observer. His best play, *Topaze* (1928), was a satire of the materialism and moral bankruptcy of postwar French society, though with *Marius* (1929), the first instalment of the *trilogie marseillaise*, he had already begun to exploit the rich vein of Provençal tragicomedy which was to become his stock in trade. The advent of *le parlant*, the 'talkies', persuaded him that cinema, freer to move in time and space than stage-bound theatre, offered exciting possibilities as a new and 'total' form of dramatic art. He ceased to think of himself as a playwright and staked all on becoming a man of the cinema. Between 1933 and 1940 he made a dozen films, all set in working class Marseilles or the hills above his native Aubagne, which were not only immensely popular with cinema audiences everywhere but are now regarded highly as fine examples of the cinema director's art. However, the defeat of France in June 1940 imposed severe constraints on film production. There were shortages of film stock, travel restrictions and severe problems of finance even in the Free Zone, while, in the Occupied Zone, the Germans were prepared to authorise the making of only those films which conformed to strict censorship procedures.

When France was overrun, Pagnol halted the filming of *La Fille du puisatier*, which had begun in the Midi in May. It was completed in August, and when released in December its implicit message of patriotism was well received. He started work on a new project, but practical difficulties (always scientifically-minded, Pagnol even attempted to manufacture his own film stock) led him to abandon *La Prière aux étoiles*, which was never completed. Refusing to participate in the

Comité d'Organisation de l'Industrie Cinématographique, a body created by the Germans to co-ordinate French film production, Pagnol finally withdrew to a sequestered retreat in the hills of Provence, where he enlivened his forced inactivity by reading and by working on film scripts.

The significance of his decision to keep the lowest of profiles must be measured against the reactions of other prominent film people. Some stars like Gabin escaped to the U.S.A., and a number of France's major film directors—Jean Renoir, René Clair and Julien Duvivier—watched events from Hollywood, where they continued to work, projecting an image of France which they believed contributed in some way to the war effort. A larger number—Danielle Darrieux, Maurice Chevalier, Jean-Louis Barrault and the *cinéaste* Marcel Carné, for example—remained behind for a variety of reasons: some believed that by staying they could help keep up morale, while others found it impossible to work in any language but French. Though Pagnol had a degree in English, he too could not face the thought of working abroad. But neither was he prepared to work while France was occupied. Of those who remained, Pagnol was one of the few major figures in the film industry who chose to maintain a dignified silence during the war years.

After the Liberation, during the *épuration*, many old scores were settled against those suspected of collaboration. Public figures in the entertainment industry were particularly vulnerable and Pagnol, newly chosen as the President of the *Société des Auteurs*, carried out an unappetizing task with good-humoured fairness. In 1945, he married the actress Jacqueline Bouvier and made *Naïs*, from a Zola short story. The following year he was elected to the Académie Française, the first film director to be so honoured. He took his duties with great seriousness and embarked upon undertakings consistent with his new status as an 'intellectual'. Always proud of his education and his connection with *l'université*, he turned *Hamlet* into French, began a translation of Virgil's *Bucolics* (which appeared in 1957) and published *Notes sur le rire* (1947) and a somewhat bad-tempered tract, *La Critique des critiques* (1949), which denounced ill-founded and insensitive criticism and settled old scores.

In a sense, Pagnol was trying to move his career in a new

direction. He did not abandon cinema, however, and made a biography of Schubert, *La Belle Meunière* (1948), and two years later released his second attempt at *Topaze* and an adaptation of a Maupassant *conte*, *Le Rosier de Mme Husson*, both starring Fernandel. But his experience of postwar cinema was not a happy one: cinema audiences now demanded a harder-edged realism and his experiments with technicolor processes ran into technical difficulties. In the 1930s he had exercised total control over every aspect of production, a luxury made impossible by the new austerity. Moreover, the famous 'team' of actors and technicians which had constituted the 'Pagnol family' had dispersed: he had become estranged from Orane Demazis, and the great Raimu died in 1946. By 1950, Pagnol was still looking for ways of re-establishing himself.

That year, he began work on a new script entitled *Manon des sources*. It was based on an anecdote which he had heard from an old shepherd many years before when holidaying as an adolescent in the hills above Aubagne. An 'étranger de la ville' had brought his family to live on the farm of 'Lou Gibous' which he had inherited. Before they arrived, a neighbour, who had for many years wanted the farm for himself, blocked the spring without which the property was unworkable, uninhabitable and worthless. The entire population of the nearby village were aware of what was afoot, but stood by in silence as they watched the unfortunate 'étranger' kill himself hauling water for his crops. No one was prepared to reveal the existence of the spring because 'it was none of their business'.

Maupassant or the Zola of *La Terre* would have turned this sordid anecdote into a bitter tale of peasant greed. Pagnol, with a temperament as sunny as it was serious, saw other possibilities in the sorry fate of the 'étranger' and used it as the basis for one of his funny-sad commentaries on human existence. *Manon des Sources*, shot at La Treille in two months during the summer of 1952, proved a worthy successor to his 'Provençal Saga' films of the 1930s. But the film also looked forward to *L'Eau des collines*. For his novel, Pagnol was to recast the shepherd's story and alter the emphasis significantly. *Manon des sources* was the first fruit of a creative process which spans a dozen years. The richness and complexity of

L'Eau des collines will emerge with much greater clarity if we
begin, as Pagnol did, in the cinema.

*****

The action takes place in and around Les Bastides Blanches
and occupies a few weeks in July. Though the village has the
'timeless' quality of films like *Angèle* or *Regain*, which are set
vaguely in the twenties, a stray reference to the atomic bomb
indicates that the setting is post-1945. From the terrace of the
café, the butcher, the carpenter, the mayor, old Papet, Maurice,
the *instituteur*, and Monsieur Belloiseau, a lawyer's clerk who
has retired to the village, follow the progress of a manhunt,
news of which is relayed by Ange, *le fontainier*, who keeps
watch from the church steeple. Two policemen and a sergeant
are chasing Manon, 'the goat-girl', who has been accused of
assaulting Polyte, one of the village adolescents. Maurice
learns that Manon is also known locally as 'la fille aux sources'
and that she is the daughter of a 'bossu' who had come many
years before from the town with his wife, an unsuccessful
professional singer, to settle on the farm of Les Romarins. Both
their children, Paul and Manon, had been born on the farm but
the lack of a natural water supply had meant daily treks to a
distant spring, back-breaking toil and grinding poverty. The
villagers had not taken to them and the *bossu* was too diffident
to make the first friendly overtures. Only Ugolin, old Papet's
nephew, had been prepared to help, though his overtures of
friendship had been far from disinterested. Ugolin, who had
designs on the farm, had spread word that the 'étranger' was
from Peypin, the traditional enemy of Les Bastides Blanches,
and for good measure added that anyone who went near Les
Romarins would probably be shot at.

Two years previously, Paul, then fifteen, had drunk bad
water from the well at Les Romarins, caught a fever and died.
A month later, the *bossu* went out into his dry fields, lay down
on the parched earth and simply gave up the unequal struggle.
He had mortgaged the farm to pay for medicines for his son,
and the property was auctioned off to Ugolin. Manon and her
mother, who had gone into a decline after Paul's death, were
forced to leave and settle in a cave in an isolated cliff on a

barren and therefore worthless part of their property. With them went Baptistine, an aged Piedmontese widow whom they had befriended.

Maurice learns further that, within days of acquiring the property, Ugolin had rediscovered the spring at Les Romarins which had been 'lost' and which the villagers always knew existed but had never mentioned. They were too busy scraping a living from the arid soil, and in any case believed that the *bossu* would have found it for himself had he been a true peasant and not a townsman with foolish ideas. But when the mayor now repeats what his dying sister had told him only two months earlier, that the *bossu* was in fact the son of Florette Camoins from whom he had inherited Les Romarins, and therefore not an *étranger* at all, old Anglade, Pamphile the carpenter, the butcher Clarius and the rest begin to feel uncomfortable. Only old Papet is unrepentant: the bossu was 'un prétentieux' and Ugolin did nothing wrong in buying the property which he had since successfully used for growing carnations.

In the hills, Manon takes her leave of Baptistine, who has cursed the village: her husband's grave has been desecrated on expiry of the five-year period which had guaranteed him rest in the cemetery at Les Bastides Blanches. She urges Manon to leave too, but Manon, who already knows most of the facts about Ugolin's treachery and the silent complicity of the villagers, has resolved to take her revenge. She has no clear idea of what to do, and for the moment is content to follow the lead of Carmen, in Bizet's opera, who drove men mad with love. Earlier that day, she had cracked the skull of Polyte, who had made advances to her, and was there not some poor fool whom she sometimes heard shouting his love for her across the echoing hills? But fleet of foot though Manon may be, the bells of her goats give her away and she is captured.

The story of the struggles and death of Jean de Florette emerges slowly, but the mood in which it is told is comic—Monsieur Belloiseau's deafness is exploited to the full—and the farcical quality of these early scenes may be gauged by the discomfiture of Ange, whose wife, Amélie, hurls the family stew out of the window, one of the few incidents which survive in the novel. The same comic mood dominates the mock trial of Manon, presided over by the pompous police sergeant, who fancies himself as a judge. Defended by Maurice, Manon is acquitted of assault, and the more serious matter of the theft of crops is dropped when Ugolin refuses to press charges. But the hearing also allows Pagnol to show the naivety, cunning and greed of the villagers, and he gives some vintage comic lines to minor characters. The proceedings are brought to a close when Monsieur Belloiseau's hearing aid explodes.

Free once more, Manon returns to the hills where she meets Baptistine, who is leaving for Aubagne. Before she goes, she gives Manon the means of revenging herself on the village: the secret of the spring in a hidden grotto which feeds the fountain at Les Bastides. Having thus been handed the weapon she has been looking for, Manon decides to block the spring and leave the area to find work in the tile factory at Aubagne, as she tells Maurice whom she meets on one of his geological expeditions. She speaks freely of her family and he is most understanding. When Ugolin follows her and offers her marriage, she is sickened, but nevertheless continues to lead him on.

At a ceremony to commemorate the generosity of Ernest Lacombe, an 'étranger de la ville' who had bequeathed a sum of money enabling water from a mountain spring to be piped directly to the village, Monsieur Belloiseau makes a long and very funny speech which continues even though the fountain suddenly runs dry. In the general panic, Manon is accused of witchcraft and the water engineer is summoned. To the assembled town councillors—in the novel, he speaks to a general meeting—he explains in words 'longs d'un kilomètre' that he does not know why the water has stopped and guesses that it may never return. Éliacin, as in the novel, demands the water he has paid for and is ejected with difficulty. Manon, who is present to observe the panic which she knows will follow the failure of the water supply, tours the village and witnesses unpleasant scenes of peasant selfishness. Already some villagers are preparing to abandon their homes and move away from the area.

The sermon preached by the *curé* (which lasts a full seventeen minutes) leads not to the heart-searching which he intended but to the search for the person who was responsible for bringing calamity upon the population, for the view is widely held that the water has been cut off by God as a punishment for the guilty. In a highly-charged meeting in Maurice's garden, Ugolin's role in the death of Jean de Florette is publicly revealed. But the villagers realise that by keeping silent they too must share the blame. Rejected by Manon and with his villainy finally exposed by Éliacin, who saw him block the spring, Ugolin returns to Les Romarins where he sees the ghosts of Jean and his family. He writes his will, in which he leaves the farm to Manon, and hangs himself, the victim, as Papet says, of unrequited love and his unfortunate heredity.

The mayor, Anglade, Éliacin, Pamphile and the rest of the villagers climb up to Manon's mountain home with peace offerings. Their change of heart comes late in the day, but they mean well and their repentance is sincere. At first, Manon rejects their gifts, viewing them as ignoble bribes intended to persuade her to join the procession which they hope will placate Heaven, the only power capable of restoring the water supply. But such is the delicacy of feeling shown by old Anglade and Claudius, the butcher—Pagnol exploits the sentimentality of the situation to the full—that she finally comes to see that they genuinely regret maintaining a sinful silence when they might have performed a good action. She agrees to take part in the procession which, through the intercession of Saint Dominique, will perhaps give them back their water and allow the village to live.

Maurice, however, has long suspected that Manon knows more about the village water supply than she has revealed. Now that Ugolin is dead, Les Romarins is hers, and the village has in effect acknowledged the collective crime of silence. When she confesses that she blocked the spring, Maurice has little trouble in persuading her to undo what she has done and, armed with picks, they set off together for the secret grotto.

The following day Manon also confesses to the *curé*, who refuses to halt the procession. Although the water may have been cut off by human rather than divine intervention, a miracle has occurred, for not only have the villagers been forced to examine their consciences, but Manon has been spared a lifetime of the guilt she would have borne had she killed the whole village by remaining silent when she might have done a good deed. In a dramatic climax, the water returns and the villagers run off to tend their plants.

Anglade buys what remains of Ugolin's crop and Manon is now rich. She abandons her plan to live in Aubagne and will marry Maurice.

* * * * *

To anyone who has read *L'Eau des collines*, Pagnol's film will come as a surprise. The basic situation is immediately recognisable and certain characters will be familiar. But the events, the mood and even the settings are very different. The tale of Jean de Florette's struggle and death is not told directly, but emerges incidentally as the motivation for Manon's revenge. Manon and Ugolin (though he is thirty-nine) survive the change of medium, and we recognise Philoxène, Pamphile, Éliacin the Mighty, Ange the *fontainier*, Amélie and the *curé*. But the character and role of others are quite foreign. Old Anglade is given much more opportunity to show his piety, and the genial and likeable Claudius, the butcher, is given the task of restoring our faith in human nature. And Baptistine, far from being the bystander of the novel, is given a crucial role in the plot: it is she who discovers the secret grotto which enables Manon to avenge her father and brother. Maurice (who later becomes Bernard) plays a dominant role from the start, and it is through his eyes that we come to understand the situation and see how it might be resolved. Monsieur Belloiseau figures prominently, and Pagnol clearly relies heavily on him to lift the tone out of the implicit tragic mode into a vein of farcical comedy, which is further served by the pomposity of the police sergeant. On the other hand, Aimée never appears at all and, more important, Papet is a minor figure. Furthermore, he has a sister and daughters of his own: though he descends from 'une famille de pendus', he and Ugolin are far from being 'the last of the Soubeyrans'.

These major differences in the cast lead to differences in the texture of the drama. Monsieur Belloiseau and the police sergeant are clearly comic figures, and the large roles which they are given suggest that Pagnol was primarily concerned with exploiting the humour of the situation. There are scenes of broad farce, few of which survive in the novel. There is, too, a vein of cosy sentimentality—notably in the expiation scene in Manon's mountain fastness—which enables Pagnol to project a view of the villagers that is considerably more lenient than in the written version. If Pagnol opted to amuse and forgive, he also chose not to pursue the darker implications of his tale. The tragedy of Manon's parents is underplayed, or rather it is trivialised, the death of Paul in particular being a somewhat maudlin invention. The emphasis falls here less upon the defeat of idealism than upon Manon's vengeance. There is no suggestion that Jean is a dreamer: at one point, Manon even remarks that he considered rabbits to be vermin, like rats. Ugolin's equally idealistic vision of fields of flowers, which will help to make him human in *L'Eau des collines*, is never mentioned, with the result that he appears more limited, grasping and selfish than in the later version, and his wronging of Manon becomes, in moral terms, much more clear-cut. In their later incarnations, both Manon and Ugolin are far more fully and satisfyingly drawn.

In spite of the *jettatura* cast by Baptistine and the superstitious reactions of the villagers, there is nothing mysterious in the resolution of the story. For Maurice, events are to be explained quite simply in human terms, and he takes the view that the largely illiterate villagers behave as they do because they are all too predictably conditioned by peasant greed and superstitition. He also reasons that Jean too must share part of the blame: 'Les victimes ne sont jamais tout à fait innocentes. Il a eu le tort d'être ce qu'il était dans un milieu qui n'était pas le sien' (*Manon des sources*, Éditions Pastorelly, 1984, p. 331). He never told the Bastidiens who he was, and never made a move to show that he wanted their friendship: 'Mon père n'était pas raisonnable', admits Manon (*ibid.*, p. 276). It may be true that Jean was held back less by pride than by his natural diffidence, but he was clearly part of the equation: his character was his fate. Even the *curé* is anxious to play down the 'miracle' which restores water and life to the dying village. Manon's revenge, he says, forced his parishioners to examine their moral selves, and her change of heart saved her from a great burden of guilt—a rather humanistic interpretation which discards the intervention of the Almighty,

who appears not as a divine power but as a sort of moral
umpire: 'Les vrais miracles, c'est dans les âmes que Dieu les
fait' (*ibid.*, p. 339). Ugolin's death is likewise reduced to human
terms. He was driven to suicide, observes Maurice, by his
heredity, remorse amd love: 'C'était une âme obscure et
violente, qui n'a connu que les passions. Il a renoncé à la vie
pour obtenir votre pardon' (*ibid.*, p. 332). Manon suggests that
his death was 'un crime devant Dieu', but Maurice persists in
underplaying the supernatural solution: 'Il s'est terriblement
puni lui-même, et les autres sont pleins de remords' (*ibid.*, pp.
332-3). If the mode is comic, the mood is humanistic and Pagnol
directs us to the conclusion that events are to be explained in
terms of the chemistry of the situation. The notion of justice
which he puts forward remains resolutely of this world.

While some elements of the exposition—Pétugue's
explanation of how he first saw Manon in the graveyard, the
engineer's report, the fury of Éliacin, the *curé*'s sermon and the
inquisition on Maurice's terrace—remain more or less intact,
events and incidents are for the most part presented quite
differently. Manon's blocking and unblocking of the spring in
the secret grotto are not shown in the film, though they
generate considerable drama in the novel. And overall, the
story unfolds in the village, so that the mysterious presence of
the Provençal countryside, which has a profound influence
upon what happens in the novel, becomes a somewhat insipid
backdrop to what is essentially a kind of 'étude de mœurs
paysannes'. One or two reviewers sensed that behind the story
lay 'quelque chose de biblique et d'homérique', but also noted
that the subject had been treated 'sur le ton le plus familier'.

In its own terms, *Manon des sources* is a hugely
entertaining film which is no less profound and moving than
the films Pagnol had made of peasant life in the 1930s. But it
was not a success, for a number of reasons. The final version
ran to nearly four hours, and its length alone alarmed
distributors, who did not respond favourably to Pagnol's
suggestion that it should be shown in two separate parts,
Manon des sources and *Ugolin*. In the event, it was severely
cut for commercial distribution and failed to make the impact
which Pagnol had hoped for. But there was worse. At a time
when cinema was dominated by Hollywood musicals, tough

film noir and violent realism, the tone and subject of the film proved to be unfashionable. It seemed that Pagnol had outstayed his welcome in the cinema.

Chapter Two

Film to Book

In 1954, the year after the release of *Manon des sources*, Pagnol completed *Les Lettres de mon moulin*, a screen adaptation of four of Alphonse Daudet's tales of Provençal life and legend which first appeared in 1869. It was a labour of love into which Pagnol injected a great deal of his own half-ironic affection for the manners and landscape of his native Midi. But though the critics were respectful, what was to prove to be Pagnol's last film was given a muted reception. It was pronounced too wordy, too literary and too long. Pagnol had misjudged the mood of the times and had again failed to impress the distributors, who preferred the more manageable length of ninety minutes. *Les Lettres de mon moulin* was severely pruned for showing—a prologue and one whole tale were cut altogether—but the film failed to make the impact which Pagnol had hoped for. His experience of the new men of cinema made it quite clear to him that his goals and methods as a film director were no longer seasonable. Perhaps too his stock in trade of comic Provençal drama had lost its appeal in the more cynical climate of the fifties. He began casting round for new openings for his talents.

His 1954 translation of *Hamlet* had received excellent notices when it was performed at the Avignon festival, and Pagnol now resolved to return to the theatre. On 6 October 1955, the first performance took place of *Judas*, a reworking of the story of the betrayal of Christ. Many thought it a strange choice of subject from the pen of an author principally known as a lightweight entertainer, while to others Pagnol's charitable interpretation of the role and character of Judas was theologically surprising, even shocking. But it was neither the novelty of the subject matter nor the controversial defence of Judas's act which led to Pagnol's first spectacular failure in over twenty-five years. Nor were production difficulties to blame, though in its short run two actors playing Judas were taken seriously ill. The reason was the play itself, which is quite uncharacteristically earnest and turgid. Pagnol had clearly intended to lighten the mood by jokily updating the situation (the soldiers talk about pensions and use regional accents and modern slang), but he succeeded only in being patronising. Much to Pagnol's dismay, the play closed after a few weeks. He had always taken the view that the verdict of the paying public is final, but he was both pained and puzzled by the reaction of critics and audiences. Some of his greatest successes had been written quickly, he said afterwards, but he had laboured long and hard over *Judas*, and it had brought him only the bitter taste of defeat.

Flawed though it may be as a play, *Judas* is nevertheless worth considering seriously, for it reveals the depths of Pagnol's moral preoccupations and is directly relevant to the underlying themes of both *Manon des sources* and *L'Eau des collines*.

For centuries Judas has been viewed as the man who betrayed Christ for money. But, argued Pagnol (as had others before him), Judas enjoyed a high rank among the disciples and was chosen as their treasurer. It hardly seems likely, then, that he would sell his master for the trifling sum of thirty pieces of silver when he had daily opportunities of embezzling far larger amounts from the common purse. Some theologians too have been struck by the meagreness of the 'avarice' solution and have alternatively argued that Judas's act was motivated by a desire to force Jesus into proclaiming himself openly as the Son of God or, more mundanely, into giving a signal to the population of Jerusalem who would then rise against the Roman yoke and accept Christ as their revolutionary leader. Pagnol dismisses this argument too, and instead adopts the view of Peter (*Acts*, i: 16), who declared that: 'It was needful that the scripture should be fulfilled'. According to Pagnol, Judas was a loyal friend and faithful disciple. Yet it was written that Jesus would be betrayed. Therefore there was need of one to betray. It was the destiny of Judas to carry out the act which 'fulfilled the scripture'.

Pagnol's Judas is a far cry from the false friend and sneaking betrayer of tradition. He is an idealist caught up in a chain of

circumstances beyond his control. How can he be guilty if he is
the instrument of God's will? He believes that he has been
chosen as the agent of Providence, that he is bound by the
chains of the prophets and that he has no control over his fate.
But if he submits, reluctantly at first and then with growing
conviction, he does not do so blindly and unquestioningly. He
never ceases to believe that Jesus is the Messiah, but makes the
mistake of trying to impose his own terms upon events. He
gladly accepts the opprobrium that will always be associated
with his name, but he persuades himself that Jesus will not die:
by some miracle He will proclaim His divinity and the trial will
be an opportunity offered to human justice to understand and
repent. Judas comes to believe that he has been chosen to bear
the burden of sin of all mankind and that his shameful act is
necessary for the salvation of the world. In other words, he
casts himself in the role of sacrificial victim who is charged
with a sacred mission. So when Christ dies on the cross, it is he
who feels betrayed: for all his good intentions, he has served
'the cruelty of the Lord'. In other words, Judas emerges as the
well-meaning victim of a situation not of his making.

Yet at the same time he is not entirely blameless, for by
attaching conditions to his collaboration—his refusal to believe
that his role will be that of a mere traitor and his assumption
that it is honourable, even heroic—he is guilty of the sin of
pride. Had he known that the scriptures would indeed be
fulfilled literally, he says, he would have torn them up and
refused to denounce Jesus. In other words, Judas, like Manon's
father, is an idealist who is 'prétentieux' and 'pas raisonnable'.
It is as an example of 'le malheur innocent' that the Roman
centurion, who pronounces Pagnol's verdict at the end of the
play, commends his soul to God: 'Pardonnez-lui son orgueil,
ayez pitié de son désespoir, et recevez dans votre miséricorde
celui qui a peut-être mal compris la consigne, mais qui a cru
vous obéir'. Judas's tragedy is therefore that of the idealist,
who seeks to rewrite the inevitable by attempting to bend
reality to fit his view of how things ought to be rather than
accepting them as they are. Manon is saved from making
exactly the same mistake when she is persuaded to abandon
her vengeance and redeem the village. But the Jean de Florette
of L'Eau des collines, who is no less convinced than Judas that

he can give reality the shape of his dreams, will die for succumbing to the same error.

Although quite different in mood, treatment and subject from the funny-sad chronicles of Provence for which he was best known, *Judas* clearly remains very much a province of Pagnol country. It is a play which once again charts with sympathy and understanding the plight of a victim who is not wholly innocent. Judas may be more of a thinker than most of Pagnol's other victims, but his faults are the same. He is guilty of pride, certainly, but there is no malice in him. His act is not motivated by any thought of gain or advantage, but by a naive and rather touching sense of his own importance, an all too human failing which Pagnol was always ready to defend. It is because his death results from the tragedy of good intentions that Pagnol ultimately judges him worthy, not of blame or censure, but of pity.

The subject of *Judas* articulates in an unusually direct form a dilemma to which Pagnol returned again and again throughout his career. The unity of his whole *œuvre* derives from a preoccupation with the conflict between human desire and the spoiling power of existence. If there is a single theme which runs through the whole of his work, it is a concern for innocence, constantly under threat in a hostile world. In the indignant, satirical comedies which Pagnol had staged during the twenties, opposition came mainly from the corruption of society. When Kid Marc, the boxer of *Un direct au cœur* (1925), learns that the string of victories which have earned him a crack at the title were not honestly won but fixed by his crooked manager, he is forced into choosing between withdrawing and protecting his integrity, or fighting and collaborating with a system which he knows to be rotten. The same dilemma faces Topaze, the ingenuous teacher, dismissed for being too honest, who by accident finds himself in a position to become wealthy by manipulating the same economic system which denied Kid Marc the luxury of maintaining his integrity intact. On this level, Pagnol's concept of human destiny is strictly non-metaphysical: the plight of his characters results from the gulf which separates their unrealistically pure moral natures from the facts of social existence. Indeed, Pagnol lays part of the blame upon them and accuses them of clinging to an outmoded, literal-minded concept of honesty which ensures that they will be unhappy. Their allegiance to a very strict sense of duty frustrates their legitimate ambitions—for Kid Marc dearly wants to be champion and Topaze freely admits to wanting success—and prevents them from being true to themselves: it is only when Bachelet, in *Les Marchands de gloire* (1925), lowers his moral standards that he feels free to 'vivre son véritable personnage'. Bachelet, Kid Marc and Topaze are all innocents at odds with the moral values of the postwar world of the twenties. Pagnol, who appears to have shared their unease, allows them to choose success against adherence to strict ethical values.

Not surprisingly, Pagnol was accused of cynicism, and indeed had he preached nothing more than the abandonment of traditional values in favour of a doctrine of material success, the charge would have been amply justified. But in reality his concern for innocence had already reached much further than the clash between the old morality and the laxer ethical trends of the modern world. *Jazz* (1926) told the story of Blaise, a professor of Greek, whose life has been devoted to scholarship and the disinterested pursuit of knowledge. By chance, new materials are discovered which completely discredit his work and, realising that he has wasted his youth in worthless effort, he shoots himself, the unhappy victim of circumstance. Here, innocence is not attacked by any kind of fashionable immorality but by chance, or perhaps more accurately, by Fate. The idea that there is a force which is opposed to human will and happiness reappears in *Marius*, where the hero's wanderlust casts a sombre pall over the love he feels for Fanny. Throughout the Marseilles 'trilogy' of *Marius* (1929), *Fanny* (1931) and *César* (1936), innocent desires are consistently thwarted by forces over which they have no control: César can never be the grandfather he longs to be, nor is Panisse ever more than a substitute father, and Marius and Fanny will probably never find happiness together. Yet they do not act out of wickedness, nor do they deliberately set out to hurt others: at most they are foolish and as such they deserve pity. Fate, chance or accident prevents them all from achieving their simple desires, and none succeeds in living 'son véritable personnage'.

Pagnol, who was not a religious man in any conventional sense, never explained what he meant by 'fate', though during the thirties the thwarting of human happiness is regularly expressed no longer in social terms, but exclusively through what might be called a pagan appreciation of nature. It is present in the way love enters hearts unbidden and wreaks havoc in the lives of bystanders. It emerges out of the hills and valleys of the Provençal landscape, which constitutes not merely the setting of Pagnol's tales but a presence endowed with a mysterious power to shape the lives of those who see their simple desires denied or fulfilled according to the caprice of their destinies. A number of factors clearly contributed to the philosophy (perhaps intuition is a better word) that life is unpredictable and human happiness precarious. Pagnol's closeness to the arid hills of the Provence he loved, his knowledge of its moods and sudden changes, his keen sense of its beauty and cruelty, confirmed what the Latin authors he loved had divined two thousand years earlier: that man is the plaything of the gods, and that his desires are granted or refused according to no discernible system of human values or divine justice. In all things, nature rules. It was just such a view, projected with atmospheric intensity, which he found in the work of his compatriot Jean Giono. Pagnol adapted four Giono tales and novels and turned them into highly successful films—*Jofroi* (1934), *Angèle* (1934), *Regain* (1937) and *La Femme du boulanger* (1938)—which significantly modified the openly magical, poetic tone of the originals. For while Pagnol's attitudes stemmed from a fundamentally pessimistic view of life, he was prevented from acquiring a truly tragic vision by his resilient personality which enabled him to sympathise with the doomed, rejoice with the elect and set the whole farce in a perspective of amused stoicism. It is precisely this mixture of the tragic and the comic which explains much of his lasting popularity with the public.

With *Judas*, however, he had for once departed significantly from the formula, and his new, more directly didactic seriousness had struck no chord with audiences. Eager to make up for his failure, Pagnol took little persuading to try again. On 28 September 1956 he staged *Fabien*, which closed after only a hundred performances: it was an even more serious setback.

Though Pagnol continued to regard *Fabien* with affection, it is difficult to see why. The play was not new, though it had been considerably revised, for it was in about 1928 that he turned an anecdote told by a friend into a 'comédie gaie' which is neither comic nor light-hearted. Fabien is a seedy fairground photographer, adored by Milly, who is enormously fat and totally, slavishly devoted to him. When Milly's sister, Marinette, comes to stay, the inevitable happens and Marinette becomes pregnant. Milly is profoundly hurt and prepares to leave, but when the doctor announces that Marinette is not pregnant after all, it is Marinette who leaves, and Fabien has no trouble in persuading Milly to stay as though nothing had happened. The plot is preposterous, the main characters are either unpleasant or unbelievable, and the mood is grotesque, cruel even. The Bearded Lady, the Bird Man, the Human Giant and the rest of the fairground people are shown as freaks and are exploited in the worst possible taste, while Pagnol's condescending attitude to Milly uncovers a far from attractive streak of misogyny.

Yet *Fabien*, the bleakest of all Pagnol's works, is another illustration of his pessimistic view of the human condition. Milly is doomed to unhappiness because she was not born under a lucky star. Like the 'sympathique idiot' characters played by Fernandel in the 'Provençal Saga' films, she is in love with a person who in looks and intelligence is manifestly beyond her reach. Once again Pagnol asserts his belief that there is a natural order of things which, whatever our hopes or desires, will inevitably assert itself. Nor is Providence prepared to reward Milly's patient devotion: she longs for a child but it is her sister, who has no maternal feelings, who becomes pregnant. Yet, seen objectively, the apportioning of blame becomes problematic: 'Elle a raison, c'est la victime', says the sweet-seller, though he adds immediately that Fabien and Marinette, who are young and in love, are not altogether to blame for what has happened. It is life that is unfair. There are always casualties in love for 'les grands événements de notre vie ne dépendent pas de nous, puisqu'ils sont inscrits dans les astres. C'est là-haut que tout est réglé d'avance' (*Fabien*, Presses-Pocket, 1977, p. 262). Even Milly echoes this thought, though she prefers to express her stoicism in human rather than supernatural terms: 'On ne peut pas lutter contre sa nature' (*ibid.*, p. 309). Though the moral dilemma is projected into a superficial and unconvincing situation, Pagnol's message of stoicism still emerges clearly, and his sense of moral mission shines bright. As the dwarf says when it is time for the show to begin: 'Allons apprendre leur bonheur aux imbéciles en leur montrant notre malheur' (*ibid.*, p. 123).

The lessons of *Fabien* were not lost on Pagnol. One was to avoid thinking of his audience as 'imbéciles', and the other was never again to make his main character antipathetic. Without the failure of *Fabien*, in which he admitted to making this mistake, the character of Ugolin would have been much less complex and ambiguous. But the most sobering lesson of all was that Pagnol's career as a playwright was at an end. Having failed in the cinema and theatre within the space of two years, Pagnol found himself once more at the crossroads. His next expedient was to turn himself into what he modestly called 'a writer of prose'.

As a young man, he had helped found and edit a literary magazine, *Fortunio*, for which until about 1922 he had written stories like *La Fille aux yeux sombres* and a serial which he had subsequently published under the title of *Pirouettes* in 1932. His facility for writing dialogue had been the key to his success both as a dramatist and film maker, and prose narrative had long ceased to interest him. But when in 1956 he was approached by the editor of *Elle* magazine for an article about his childhood, he struck a rich vein of memory, comedy and mellow wisdom which was to start him on a new career and turn him into a much-loved classic author.

Souvenirs d'enfance (1957-60) is an artful mix of memory and invention which masquerades, none too seriously, as autobiography. Like most of Pagnol's films and plays, its origins were anecdotal. But instead of drawing upon incidents recounted to him by other people, he now thought back to his own childhood, which had been so rich in uncles, adventures and eccentricities. Unlike the serious autobiographer, he set out not to record and analyse his past, or even to tell the truth, but to recreate 'une époque disparue' in a mood of 'piété filiale'. The result was a hugely popular and quite irresistible blend of humour and shrewd observation which introduces us to his parents and follows Marcel's development until he is eleven, when he is admitted to the *lycée* at Marseilles. Pagnol never seriously planned to continue this new 'Provençal Saga' beyond his early adolescence, partly because he was an intensely private man but also because his interest, as always, lay with the problem of innocence.

Early childhood is the age of discovery, a time before the world takes on fixed patterns and rigid shapes: Marcel's hills are not simply hills, but the setting for exciting adventures, where Red Indians lurk and grizzly bears hide behind trees ready to spring upon the unsuspecting trapper. By the time Marcel begins secondary school at the start of *Le Temps des secrets*, he knows that his innocence is lost and gone forever: 'L'expérience, la "précieuse" expérience, avait désenchanté mes collines, et dépeuplé les noires pinèdes: plus de lion, plus d'ours grizzly, pas même un loup-cervier solitaire. Ils avaient tous réintégré les pages illustrées de mon *Histoire naturelle* et je savais bien qu'ils n'en sortiraient jamais plus' (*Le Temps des secrets*, p. 32). Growing up means the dimming of the child's ability to live in a magical world, and the process of disenchantment led Pagnol to restate his conviction that life is hostile to innocence. In 1928, as a commentary on the experiences of Topaze, he had quoted a chance remark made by his barber: 'La société, voyez-vous monsieur, si elle continue, elle tuera les justes'. In *Le Château de ma mère*, his father's moral uprightness exposes him to the bullying of the guard who patrols the grounds which the family uses as a short cut. Being in the wrong, he capitulates: 'Comme on est faible quand on est dans son tort,' he sighs. But the older Pagnol corrects him: 'La vie m'a appris qu'il se trompait, et qu'on est faible quand on est pur' (*Le Château de ma mère*, pp. 270; 272). If Topaze was undone by society, Joseph is undermined by his own goodness. In other words, Pagnol's autobiography is another meditation upon the 'just' and the 'pure' as they struggle to retain their integrity in a world which is eternally hostile to their innocent natures.

His father's humiliation (which is as much an illustration of his inoffensive nature as the 'glory' which his hunting exploit brings him) may seem to be a trifling circumstance on which to erect a moral truth. But Pagnol introduces soberer and graver memories which connect the defeat of innocence with a more general view of the arbitrariness of existence, seemingly so often opposed to our finest ideals and, in the long run, destructive of hope and happiness. Marcel's friend Lili was killed in the trenches in 1917; his brother Paul was to die in 1932; and, above all, his mother succumbed to illness in 1910. All that remained of those far-off days was a handful of happy memories and a burden of sorrow. 'Telle est la vie des hommes. Quelques joies, très vite effacées par d'inoubliables chagrins.' It would be a counsel of despair, had not Pagnol added immediately: 'Il n'est pas nécessaire de le dire aux enfants' (*Le Château de ma mère*, p. 304).

The afterthought is important for it not only defines Pagnol's philosophy very clearly but reveals his stance as a manipulator of destinies. Behind it lies a fund of pessimism, even of fatalism, but Pagnol's stoicism overcomes any real sense of tragedy. He stands above his characters towards whom he adopts a consistently paternalistic attitude, rather in the manner of Dickens, whom he much admired. He shows genuine affection for all of them, even for the unpleasant Fabien, and, as it were, watches them like a father who observes his offspring at play. Some survive happily, others fall down and hurt themselves. Whenever he can, he rescues them from their folly. But when they are beyond help he lets them go, for if he is to be true he can have no licence to prevent the inevitable.

Pagnol's quest to re-establish his reputation had ended rather unexpectedly in a third career. As 'a writer of prose' he conquered a new generation of young readers who, if they had previously heard of him at all, knew that he was the author of plays which were occasionally revived and the maker of classic films which were to be seen only by the keenest of cinema-club goers. But just as the playwright had carried his preoccupations into the cinema, so the film maker built prose narratives around the subjects which fascinated him and the mood which his temperament dictated. Which is why, when he began writing a novel, he returned to the problem of 'le malheur innocent', the predicament of the 'pure' and the 'just', victims who are not without fault, the irresistible power of nature and the insidiousness of fate. And his overall vision remains the same. The mode is not tragic, but is rooted in an amused and tolerant stoicism which allowed him to laugh when the going was good. And Pagnol's jokes continued to be very funny indeed.

Chapter Three

Realism

The enormous success of the *Souvenirs d'enfance* was all the more gratifying because it finally gave the lie to the charge that Pagnol's career had been built, at least in part, on the efforts of other people, and in particular on those of actors like Fernandel and Raimu who had given his characters life on stage and on screen. In an interview published in *Les Nouvelles Littéraires* (16 mai 1963), he observed that: 'au théâtre—et au cinéma—l'auteur n'est pas complètement responsable de ses fours [*failures*] [...] et pas tout à fait non plus de ses succès'. But the reception of his autobiography did not merely confirm his ability to communicate in prose: it freed his voice. Fiction allowed him to speak directly to his reader:

> ... ce qu'il y a de merveilleux, c'est qu'il n'y a pas d'intermédiaires entre l'auteur et son public. Au théâtre, tu as affaire à des acteurs, à des directeurs, à des décorateurs, à tout un monde. Romancier, tu es tout ça à toi tout seul. Ton encrier, ton porte-plume et ton cahier te suffisent... Aussi, si c'est bon, à toi tout le mérite; si c'est mauvais, tu es seul responsable.

And where theatre and cinema must deal in surfaces, in suggestions of psychological reaction and motivation, the novelist is free to wander through the minds of his characters and much better equipped to conjure up, by suggestion, the colour and mood of landscapes.

Pagnol's decision to publish a novel—his first—at the age of sixty-eight was therefore based not simply on his wish to capitalise on the phenomenal success of his autobiography but also on his curiosity about a form of expression which he had hitherto neglected, even mistrusted. Just as he had welcomed the talking film as the new and total form of dramatic expression in 1930, so now he was excited by the freedom which he discovered in fiction. He was not the least interested in formal aesthetics and dismissed the 'new novels' of Robbe-Grillet, Butor and Duras, then dominating the literary scene, as an arid intellectual fashion. His allegiance went still to the likes of Dickens and Daudet, instinctive storytellers who had an eye for eccentricity, humour and human warmth.

He had not far to look when casting round for a subject. He had long sensed that he had not fully exploited the story of 'le bossu du Gibous' which had formed the basis of *Manon des sources:*

> J'avais commencé à écrire cette histoire, il y a déjà une dizaine [sic] d'années, pour en faire un film. Puis, je l'avais trouvée lugubre. Alors, le film, je l'ai fait avec un bout de la fin de l'histoire... Du temps passe. Et, un jour, par hasard, je retrouve le début tel que j'avais commencé à l'écrire. Je vois alors la chose d'un autre œil et l'idée me vient d'en faire un livre. Je me mets à écrire, à écrire, et encore une fois ça en a fait deux, de livres.

The anecdote had been merely the point of departure for Manon's vengeance, which was entirely of Pagnol's invention. The time had come for the rest of the tale to be told.

As a novelist, Pagnol breaks no new technical ground. He is perfectly happy to tell his story with the voice of the third-person, omniscient narrator, which allows him to retain full directorial control. *L'Eau des collines* is a carefully-planned novel, with carefully contrived shifts of emphasis which not only maintain our interest but create a three-dimensional picture of changing perspectives within a framework of formal realism.

It opens in an orderly fashion, like a novel by Balzac. Pagnol first gives us an overview of Les Bastides Blanches, which is built around the fountain in the square. We are then introduced to the isolated villagers who are poor, suspicious and avaricious, mind their own business and mistrust towns. Next, with the focus growing ever sharper, we meet a handful of village *notables* who put faces to the foibles and prejudices which have been evoked in general terms. Only when this scene-setting is complete does Pagnol's camera—for what we have been given thus far is the equivalent of a sequence of cinematographic 'establishing shots'—zoom in on Papet and

Ugolin, whose personal histories are sketched in some detail. But these opening pages are not significant simply for communicating the basic facts. A crucial element of this introduction is the ironic and amused tone of voice. In objective terms the characters we meet are narrow-minded and not particularly likeable. Yet from the start the narrator signals his readiness to minimise their faults by laughing at them: they are not so much wicked as foolish and ignorant. Pagnol stands above them and seems content to observe with wry tolerance, as though to imply that there is no real harm in them. His sense of the comic replaces moral judgment and, without the least hint of moralising or overt direction on his part, we are persuaded to accept his terms as a storyteller.

These seemingly artless first pages therefore serve several functions: they establish a pace which is leisurely and unhurried, they set a tone of detached but tolerant irony and they create a taste for realistic detail. The village of Les Bastides Blanches, 'two leagues from Aubagne', has clearly been located in the hills of Lower Provence. As soon as Pagnol introduces Papet, he also takes care to set his story in time. The references to a 'tilbury' and a 'boghey' have already suggested a vaguely bygone era which predates the fire-raising invasions of 'les gentils boy-scouts et les sympathiques campeurs' (J, 32). But the brief account of Papet's life—it is close on forty years since he returned from Africa in 1882 (16; 70-71)—reveals that the time is 1922, a date later confirmed by Philoxène who, now forty-seven years of age, seems to have been born in about 1874 (11; 71). The internal chronology of the novel, which carefully notes the passage of time, reveals that the action of *L'Eau des collines* occurs between 1922 and 1929, a span of seven years which curiously parallels the time between Pagnol's arrival in Paris and the staging of *Marius* which confirmed his success as a playwright. In choosing these dates, Pagnol no doubt consciously marked a return to the 'timeless' world of the 'Provençal Saga'—a time when oil lamps were still used and the mayor's telephone and the motorcar were novelties. But it may be too that he was at least half-consciously repudiating his initial account of the loss of innocence which, culminating in *Topaze*, showed the struggle between good and evil in terms of a conflict between idealism and social forces. Jean de Florette is

an 'intellectual' like Topaze, but he faces a less amenable foe
when he sets out to 'vivre son véritable personnage', for
taming nature is a taller order than beating society at its own
game. Ugolin, the floriculturist, may succeed in material terms
but he is quite unable to command Love, and while Papet
believes that he is strong because he has 'des sous', he too will
be broken by a power which takes no heed of wealth. In the
time it took the young Pagnol to abandon his early artistic
idealism and accept the rewards of his success, the
protagonists of *L'Eau des collines* work through their destinies
and face challenges which are sterner and much more final.

But the careful notation of time is only a part of Pagnol's
scrupulous realism, for the sense of place draws its strength
from very precise topographical detail. The mountains are real
mountains, the names of springs are for the most part
authentic and only the villages of Les Ombrées, Ruissatel and
Crespin are invented. 'Les Bastides Blanches' is recognisable as
the community of La Treille, with which readers of Pagnol's
autobiography will be familiar. Visitors to Aubagne are
nowadays offered guided tours of the 'Pagnol country' which
lies in a valley north of Les Camoins, and may see Le Garlaban,
the heights of Ruissatel, and the Grande Tête Rouge for
themselves. The sketch map shows the probable locations of
Les Romarins, Ugolin's 'mas de Massacan' and Manon's
'grotte du Plantier'. But topography is not Pagnol's only
concern. Long before Bernard appears on the scene, he has
informed us about the geology and orography of the region,
and he describes the flora and fauna with great exactness.
Moreover, he roots his world in a rich soil of sociological
observation. Few aspects of life in the hills remain
unexplained. We are told about the primitive tools used by the
peasants, 'dont la fonction principale était de prolonger le
manche de leurs pioches' (J, 30), we witness their poaching
techniques, and we acquire a clear idea of their agricultural
methods and working practices. It is evident that Pagnol
revelled in his close acquaintance with the hills he loved, but
the information which he supplies is never gratuitous. We need
to be able to appreciate the beauty of the hills as Jean does, and
we must know just how hard a man has to struggle to feed a
family on these dry slopes if we are to understand the enormity

of the task of reviving Les Romarins. And if we are given constant information about the climate, it is because the sun and rain play a crucial role in the drama. Hence Pagnol's insistence on the importance of water. He believed that 'Il n'y a pas de poésie en dehors des lieux communs', and accordingly described his novel as 'une histoire d'eau'. In the interview from which we have already quoted, he remarked:

> Moi, je n'ai jamais écrit que sur des lieux communs. De quoi parlent mes pièces ou mes films ? Du pain, de l'eau, de la mère, de l'enfant naturel, de choses toujours très simples.

Water is a primary socialising force: it was only when the fountain was built at Les Bastides Blanches that families scattered round about abandoned their farms and came together to form a village. In the same way, the evocation of the *garrigue* covered with *messugues*, *térébinthes*, *cades* and *gratte-cul*, and alive with *limberts* and *darnagas* (see Glossary), is not to be explained simply by a concern for authenticity and local colour: it is an essential element of Pagnol's world, where the battle for life and death emerges from the struggle to survive in an unkind landscape. The drama of *L'Eau des collines* thus acquires an epic touch and the symbolic quality of myth, for what is at stake is not only individual happiness but human civilisation itself.

As one way of giving substance to this theme, and not simply out of a scrupulous wish to be accurate, Pagnol made a serious effort to record the mentality and habits of village life. Few outside influences are of the least concern to the villagers, who have an enduring suspicion of the '"étranger[s] du dehors"' (J, 33), whom they envy for their money and whose easier life and soft 'city ways' they despise. The Bastidiens forgive 'le fils Médéric' who got on and became a customs officer; but they scorn the Testards who simply moved away because life was less difficult elsewhere (58). Papet scoffs at the 'routine' about which town-dwellers are forever complaining and he has no time for their obsession with being 'modern' (119). Self-respecting Bastidiens never actually climb to the top of any of the hills which dominate their lives, 'ces escalades inutiles' being 'un exercice sportif à l'usage des gens de la ville' (M, 57). Nor have they any use for book learning. Éliacin is barely

literate and the letters written by Ugolin, Papet and
Graffignette scarcely testify to any great level of general
culture: Papet confuses Pascal, one of the glories of French
literature, with a *fontainier* he once knew (217). They are
prepared to tolerate the garrulous Monsieur Belloiseau
because he has a knowledge of the law which he is ready to
impart without asking a fee, and they accept the *instituteur*,
because he is paid to be an 'intellectual' and therefore has an
excuse. They are prepared to listen to the water engineer, but
quickly lose faith in his learning because his impressively
polysyllabic words do not say what they want to hear. Yet
though they despise city learning and professional expertise,
they fear the long arm of officialdom. Lawyers' papers may
contain dangerous secrets and, in Papet's view, 'C'est jamais
bien raisonnable de dire au gouvernement quelque chose qu'il
ne sait pas! Ils en profitent toujours pour te mettre des impôts'
(J, 91). Narrow-minded and stubborn, they inhabit a closed
community.

Not surprisingly, though some had fought in France's wars,
they have no interest in the affairs of the world beyond their
narrow borders. Philoxène (whose name in Greek means,
ironically, 'lover of strangers') 'se disait socialiste, laïque
anticlérical, lisait ouvertement, sur sa terrasse, Le Petit
Provençal [a left-wing newspaper], et vitupérait volontiers
contre les jésuites' (J, 11). Yet as mayor of the commune and
host to the 'mécréants' who drink at his café, he is patently
ignorant of political issues, though a wily operator in his
relations with the voters and the administration. He may
detect in the *curé*'s maid 'l'espionne des Jésuites' (M, 171), and
the priest's sermon may attack the 'mécréants' as unbelievers,
but the kind of war between Republican sentiments and the
reactionary church which is depicted more forcefully in the
Souvenirs d'enfance is never allowed to intrude into the
parochial matters which are debated over a round of apéritifs
in the village's only café.

If the Bastidiens grow their own food they are also
culturally self-contained. Their morality is based on dubious
values which have the authority of tradition. Though the
women are often assertive and strong, they live in a man's
world, and while they can be more sensitive than their

chauvinist menfolk, they lend their support to common ethical
standards which are, to say the least, unorthodox. Telling lies,
pilfering and poaching are a way of life. Avoiding work in the
manner of Pique-Bouffigue, and dodging army service as
Éliacin famously does, are acceptable practices. Sexual
irregularities that are catered for locally, or in the fleshpots of
Aubagne, pass without comment. Pique-Bouffigue is justified in
killing the interloper Siméon on a number of counts: first
because the man was a stranger, secondly because he stole
from his snares ('de tous les vols, c'est le plus odieux'—J, 34),
and lastly because he has a legitimate right to revenge. Papet
batters Pique-Bouffigue without mercy for insulting his family
name, and tells lies large and small to protect his interests.
Ugolin, having stopped up Jean's water supply, generously
provides him with drinking water, and explains his conduct by
means of a highly selective ethical argument: 'D'avoir bouché
la source, c'est pas criminel: c'est pour les œillets. Mais si, à
cause de ça, il y avait des morts, eh bien peut-être qu'après
nous n'en parlerions pas, mais nous y penserions' (J, 121). The
morality of his action is clearly linked to self-interest, the basic
moral law of the Bastidiens. Pamphile has an itch to reveal the
location of the source to Jean but remains silent, because Papet
has offered him work and Papet always pays cash (242). Later,
Cabridan similarly justifies his inaction by claiming that 'j'étais
trop pauvre pour m'occuper des affaires des autres' (M, 226).
The moral code of the Bastidiens forbids them to interfere in
other people's business, and the words 'on ne s'occupe pas des
affaires des autres' recur like a refrain throughout the novel.
The new *curé* is not afraid to denounce 'l'incroyance, l'égoïsme
et l'avarice de ses paroissiens' (26), and the thrust of his sermon
is that Christian duty requires everyone to help his neighbour:
'La vertu c'est d'agir, c'est de faire le Bien' (202). Yet they turn
to whichever gods will help them in their time of need.

Exhortations to Christian virtue fall on deaf ears, for the
Bastidiens divide their faith between the established Church
and much older pagan superstitions. The villagers are only too
ready to believe in Baptistine's *jettatura*, and Manon's
familiarity with her *limbert* earns her a reputation for
witchcraft. They believe that black, long-haired dogs are
unlucky; that the dead can return to haunt the living; and that it

is dangerous to figure in other people's dreams (**M**, 87; 14; 83)). Ugolin talks timidly, deferentially to dead 'Monsieur Jean', and is quite convinced that by sewing one of Manon's ribbons to his chest he will be able to tell if his love is requited. Baptistine uses less than scientific methods to 'retirer le soleil' from the sun-struck Jean and thus demonstrates the efficacy of powers which defy conventional medicine. In this atmosphere, the *curé*'s simple faith is as powerless as Bernard's rational mind to counter the unquestioning belief in dreams, spells and magic in the hearts and minds of peasants who depend for their livelihood on their closeness to the land.

Their age-old, pagan culture is expressed in customs and traditions which Pagnol is careful to record. Papet repeats rhymes which enshrine the patterns of the weather, Jean collects old songs, and Aimée hums 'de mystérieuses musiques qui ressemblaient à celle de l'église' without actually belonging to the formal canon (J, 165). Such reminders of local lore are effectively used as indicators of the spirit of place, though they also abet Pagnol's concern to fix the people and their habitat by exploiting the linguistic landscape of Lower Provence. Les Bastides, a collection of fifty-odd red-tiled houses huddled around the fountain and the church (7), is a gossiping, squabbling world of intimate relationships which are clearly defined in the familiar names the Bastidiens give each other. Some names stress the diminutive form (Florette for Flore), while others evoke places or events (e.g., Manon des sources, Pique-Bouffigue) and family connections that would otherwise be blurred by the limited number of five or six village surnames (Ugolin de Zulma, César des Soubeyran, Manon du Bossu). The feel of their closed community emerges strongly from the language they use. Baptistine's Piedmontese (her *jettatura*, for example) is less noticeable here than in the film where her speech needed to be subtitled for French audiences, and there are only a few snatches of authentic Provençal. But the Bastidiens' vocabulary is strongly laced with non-French words. They say *chasper* (caresser) and are *estransinés* and *escagassés* when shocked. They use *espérer* for *attendre* and *graffigner* for *égratigner*. Their interjections (*Adessias, peuchère, qué, té, zou, vé, vaï!*), exclamations (*Coquin de sort! ô bonne mère!*) and insults (*fada, couillon, marrias* [vaurien]) are as aromatic as the herbs they use. But the flavour is not confined just to words: it also emerges from their fractured syntax. *Que* tends to replace all other relatives (*'mon petit, que* [dont] *je t'ai parlé hier'*) as well as *quel / quelle;* adjectives may replace nouns and even adverbs (*plantés trop profond*); reflexive verbs proliferate (*je me la garde, je me le pense*); unnecessary liaisons are made (*tu as beau-z-être conseiller*); and *y* often replaces the indirect pronoun (*donne-z-y encore un peu de soupe* for *donne-lui*). Pagnol injects into his text enough authentic Provençalisms to intensify the sense of place: his peasants do not belong at Gap or Manosque, but in Les Bastides Blanches and nowhere else.

Even so, conscious that he was writing for a national and not a local audience, Pagnol carefully measures the dose. For this reason he occasionally pauses to translate words and expressions and at times interrupts his narrative to provide short lecture notes (sometimes put into the mouth of the *instituteur*), not only about the *limbert* or the cicada (**M**, 88; 129) but also about the history and origins of words and customs. In the circumstances, it is not surprising if Pagnol's linguistic realism is restricted largely to vocabulary, and even then Yvonne Georges (*Les Provençalismes de 'L'Eau des collines'*, p. 143) has calculated that out of a count of 64,000 words in *L'Eau de collines*, only 212 boast a genuinely Provençal pedigree. If such statistical findings seem meagre, it nonetheless remains true that few authors from the area writing in French have ever dared to be as bold as Pagnol. Madame Georges further notes (pp. 182-3) that there are as many Provençal words in *L'Eau des collines* as there are in the whole work of Paul Arène (1843-1896) and significantly more than in all the writings of Alphonse Daudet (1840-1897). Even in such illustrious company, Pagnol's claims to linguistic authenticity are therefore strong.

But genuine Provençalisms are relatively unobtrusive, and rather more is achieved through the exploitation of the regional, southern French of his uneducated peasants. Their language is full of images and exaggeration, and Pagnol captures not only its rhythms but transcribes it phonetically in their letters and recreates it in speech patterns which allow the spoken word to be heard and not merely seen on the printed page: thus the Bastidiens always sound mute *e* 's (unlike those who speak with the 'accent ridicule' of Northern France—J, 33) and final consonants (*estomaque* for *estomac*, les *oss* for les *os*). Pagnol records mispronunciations (*bisteck, namerlesse, atrapénoure, lotantiques*), reproduces modified consonants (*satistiques* for *statistiques, essituteur* for *instituteur, indanité* for *indemnité*), seizes upon malapropisms like *hypothèque* (for *hypothèse*) and has a keen ear for words deformed by analogy with others, such as *entention!* for *attention!* Pagnol's careful transcription of the language of his characters gives them an earthy reality and establishes the psychological and social conditions in which their actions and reactions seem natural.

L'Eau des collines thus communicates the feel of a real world. Pagnol defines the time and describes the place in graphic detail, with the eye of a naturalist. But he is no less careful to evoke the mentality of the Bastidiens, which he anchors firmly in a carefully-judged social and linguistic frame of reference. At one level, Pagnol's realism seems designed to convey little more than a sense of the picturesque and, in his portrait of the villagers and the authentic echo of their language, to exploit a rich source of comedy. But his picture of country life has a more important effect, for the setting is not merely beautiful but natural, and his peasants are not amusing yokels but pagan savages. Their values are as hard and cruel as the barren land from which they scratch a livelihood. Beneath their foolishness and behind each prettily flowering bush lurks danger, the danger of the natural world. Pagnol's atmospheric realism establishes his tale of vengeance and blighted hopes in a setting where no quarter may be expected.

Chapter Four

Passions and Victims

Pagnol's first attempt to tell the story, for the cinema, was less atmospheric than *L'Eau des collines* was to be. This phenomenon is to be explained in part by the greater flexibility of fiction which, he discovered, was better equipped to explore character and convey the mysterious sense of place. But more important than this, the way he had first formulated events and characters for the screen was plainer and less subtle. Events had unfolded within a space of weeks and not years, and the action was situated largely in the village. As a result, the glories and menace of external nature were relegated to a place of secondary importance. Both the lack of charity and the paganism of the Bastidiens were much less heavily underlined and, although in linguistic terms Baptistine's Piedmontese and the local accent were more prominent, Pagnol was not so concerned with providing an accurate record of their language and the values which it implied as with exploiting the comic possibilities of picturesque, regional speech patterns. This, together with the interplay of farcical incident and comic characters, ensured that the overall mood of the film was dominated by Pagnol's sentimental good humour.

But if *Manon des sources* proved to be more amusing, it also turned out to be less dramatic. One obvious opportunity for generating excitement was lost because Manon's blocking and unblocking of the village's water supply occur offscreen. Her unseen act is passed over quickly in favour of the resolution of the situation: the 'miracle' happens, the village is saved, Manon will marry the *instituteur*, and the tale is brought to the cosy conclusion which the tone and mood of the film required. Moreover, from the start, Manon knows more or less how and why Ugolin acquired Les Romarins, and this too means that her gradual discovery of the truth and her growing hatred of the conniving villagers deprive the film of a source of considerable tension, one which the novel exploits to the full.

Of course the most significant difference between the screen
and the written versions of the tale is that the first volume of
L'Eau des collines relates in detail the events which have
already happened when the film opens. Pagnol's instinct as a
film maker was that the struggle and death of Jean de Florette
was too sombre for audiences: 'lugubre' was the word we have
heard him use (*supra*, p. 20). He later revised this view and
began to see the character not as weak and hopeless, but as a
vibrant eccentric whose misfortunes could be much more than
an expanded prelude to the second volume. The story of Jean
de Florette outgrew its original purpose of providing Manon
with a motive for revenge and changed the whole mood of the
second part. But to give Jean an expanded role also implied
significant changes in the role and function of other characters.
Since Manon discovers the source of the spring for herself,
Baptistine is no longer needed and is relegated to the sidelines.
Aimée, who does not appear in the film, is required to feature
in the novel as part of Jean's struggle, and Pagnol invents the
outrageous Monsieur Victor to allow her to share in Manon's
final triumph. The *instituteur*, who does not appear on the
scene until rather late in the day, ceases to be the intermediary
through whose eyes the plot unfolds, and his role is assumed by
the narrator. On the other hand, Ugolin's motives are made
much clearer, and because we know him better he ceases to be
the lonely, odd and rather unpleasant figure of the film and
becomes satisfyingly ambiguous. Most interestingly of all, old
Papet is brought centre-stage to become a major character.

But substantial changes of characterisation were not the
only innovations. Events cease to be seen from the village and
are relocated in the hills. Moreover, considerable restructuring
also became necessary. The architecture of Pagnol's film is
simple: Manon takes her revenge on Ugolin but is ultimately
saved from committing an act which would have made her as
wicked as the man who had wronged her family. The structure
of the novel is much more complex:

1.   The first phase shows the innocent ambition of Ugolin
     to make his fortune by growing flowers. He is abetted
     by old Papet, who is anxious to see his nephew renew
     the Soubeyran fortunes.

2.   Their plans are ruined by the arrival of Jean de Florette, whose equally innocent scheme to create a self-sufficient rural paradise is made impossible by Ugolin and Papet, who are prepared to stop at nothing to achieve their desires.

3.   Ugolin's enjoyment of his success continues until he is smitten with love for Manon and finally kills himself.

4.   Manon gradually pieces together the truth and resolves to take her revenge. When she falls in love, however, she ceases to punish the village.

5.   Papet, who has manipulated so many events, finally learns the futility of his actions.

It is no accident that the major phases of the story revolve around the main characters. Their shifting fortunes not only give direction and movement to the drama but explain why the emphasis moves from one to the other. These changes of focus (from Ugolin to Jean to Ugolin to Manon and finally to Papet) occur in accordance with Pagnol's own preoccupation with the fate of simple ambitions in a hostile world. His story is conceived in terms of character rather than events, and the whole of the action is rooted in the psychology of compulsive desires. Ugolin, Manon and Papet are by turn innocent and guilty, and even Jean, though he never actively seeks to harm others, exhibits a culpable obstinacy which condemns Manon and Aimée to a life of poverty and exile. But the struggle between innocence and guilt is expressed even more specifically through a series of reversals in which victims and victimisers successively swap roles. Jean's idealism turns into culpable self-delusion which ruins his family. Ugolin, the would-be flower grower, becomes the self-server who ruins Jean before becoming the victim of love. Manon's innocence turns into a thirst for vengeance which does not stop with Ugolin's death but threatens to destroy the whole of the village. And Papet, who insidiously stage-manages Jean's downfall and Ugolin's success, ends up as the plaything of fate. Maurice, the *instituteur* of *Manon des sources,* had already observed that victims are never altogether blameless. Bernard makes the same observation in the novel, where it constitutes not only the basis of Pagnol's stoicism but provides the structural framework into which the dramatic action is set. To see the principle at work, we need to see how harmless desires, when thwarted, can bring out the best and worst in Pagnol's gallery of innocents.

1. Jean de Florette

If Jean is a character added to the cast of the novel, he is not unfamiliar. He is clearly recognisable as an amalgam and extension of characters from Pagnol's earlier works. Like Marius, who heard the call of the sea, Jean is a dreamer who turns his back on the 'routine' of city life and heads for the hills where the voice of nature beckons him. But Jean is also related to Blaise and Topaze, who erroneously believed that life can be brought under control by knowledge derived from books. He has also more than a passing resemblance to the Joseph of the *Souvenirs d'enfance*. He adopts the same 'ton d'un conférencier' (J, 134) and exhibits the same blindness to his own faults, so that Ugolin's judgement of him, that he is 'plutôt prétentieux, mais sympathique' (127), could equally apply to the picture Pagnol had drawn of his father. The scene which shows Jean and his family delightedly arriving with their possessions at Les Romarins is a replay of the removal of the Pagnols to their summer village above La Treille, and young Marcel's salute to 'la gloire de [son] père' finds an echo in Manon's defence of her father's naive and trusting nature. Ugolin and Papet may have got the better of him, but 'C'était sa gloire de n'avoir pas compris la férocité de ces insectes' (M, 134). Jean is very much a member of the Pagnol family.

He considers himself to be an intellectual and prides himself on an 'infallible' memory, a sure grasp of matters both abstract and technical, and an ability to turn knowledge to practical use. Over many years he has made a study of philosophy, and is therefore not afraid to call himself, rather pompously, a 'philosopher' (J, 113). He believes absolutely that the world can be mastered by reason, book-learning and simple mathematics.

He bases his plans on weather statistics, and calculates the growth of his future rabbit population and the yield of his oriental pumpkins with an accuracy made even more absurd by his 'prudent' admonition to Aimée: 'Restons dans les limites du bon sens' (135). Not only does he believe that all problems have technical solutions, his whole view of life is distorted by a false literary perspective. His reaction when he sees his overgrown 'estate' for the first time is typical: 'C'est le Paradou de Zola!' (99). From the start, his recollection of the mysterious, abandoned garden of Eden which Zola described in *La Faute de l'abbé Mouret* (1875) comes between him and reality, and is as much a distortion as his misguided view of his dilapidated ancestral house, which for him symbolises 'toute l'antique Provence' (100). He has a faith in the myth of country life which, from Theocritus, via Rousseau in the eighteenth century through to our own obsession with the natural and the organic, has always tempted Western man. He toasts nature and the blue of the sky (108), for urban man has grown away from the land which is as much a spiritual as a physical home: Jean wants to be 'un homme de la nature'. Yet though he detests the 'routine' of city life, he has boundless faith in intellectual progress. His ambition is to tame nature by importing the latest methods and thus have the best of both worlds: he wants to be both 'moderne' and 'authentique'. He knows the theory—'il faut maîtriser l'enthousiasme en tenant à deux mains les rênes de la Raison' (138)—but is quite unable to apply it to himself. He is the eternal optimist—'D'un simple geste de la main, comme pour balayer la table, il assura instantanément la nourriture de toute sa famille' (135)—who does not doubt for an instant that nature can be shaped to fit his dreams.

His patriarchal authority—'Les femmes [...] ont toutes les qualités, sauf le bon sens!' (138)—and unbounded confidence dazzle Aimée and Manon, who find no fault with him. Others are quicker to point out his defects, and no one is readier than the narrator himself. 'Il était gentil, ce bossu, mais il n'était pas très modeste' (112). His energy is boundless and he works hard, but his plans are quite 'chimériques', for he is a dreamer (130). He blinds Ugolin with science like 'un magicien maléfique' (136) and smiles condescendingly when the 'ignorant peasant' does not grasp the scope of his plans or fails to understand his use of

words like 'massif' and 'reconnaissance' (135; 167), and his
sophisticated jokes, such as as his reference to his mother's
'bienfaisante avarice' (113). For Jean is in love with the sound
of his own voice and has a lush, polysyllabic vocabulary of
which he is more the victim than the master: he invests his
plans and surroundings with a linguistic super-reality which
abolishes obstacles, and his own word pictures convince him
that his objectives are as good as achieved. His behaviour is
compulsive, and obsession leads him to self-indulgent
contradictions. He who is forever reading moral lessons is not
above breaking the law: he imports an Australian rabbit which,
in his accident-prone care, could easily cause an ecological
disaster (184), but, like Ugolin who does not think blocking the
stream is criminal because 'c'est pour les œillets', he is quite
prepared to act against the common interest when it suits his
purpose. He is also blind to the danger of pride. Thus, though
he cuts a comic figure at Aubagne market (where is he is far too
impractical to hawk his produce unaided), he is nevertheless
'fort content de lui-même' (197). Or again, when the spectacle
of his dead crops forces him to understand that he has failed,
he cannot give up because he will not admit failure to Ugolin,
Aimée and Manon—or to himself (226). Papet shrewdly
observes his foolishness and concludes that he is 'un innocent
de la ville' (118). Courageous he might be, but 'c'est un homme
qui lit les livres, et qui a de l'ambition... Ça mène bien loin [...],
et c'est ça qui le perdra' (201).

On the other hand, Pagnol takes good care to show why
even Ugolin finds him genuinely 'sympathique'. Jean acts with
great kindness to Baptistine and he has a boundless,
philosophical trust in his fellow man: he thinks the best of
Ugolin, the good neighbour, even though first Manon (who
instinctively thinks of him as a toad—149) and later Aimée
come to dislike him intensely. Misguided and self-deluding
though he might be, there is nevertheless something admirable,
even heroic, in the way he sets about shaping reality to fit his
dreams. Even Papet commends his courage. He adapts well to
his new life, learns new skills and shows due reverence for the
creatures he sees around him, especially since 'aucune de ces
créatures vivantes ne savait qu'il était bossu' (157). For his
bosse is his burden. On one of the rare occasions we seem him

go to Les Bastides Blanches, he believes that Médéric is laughing at his deformity, though in reality he attracts attention because he is absurdly overdressed (204). His sensivity to his misshapen physique increases his isolation, for it prevents him from making friendly overtures to the villagers. It is only when he carries water that his *bosse* serves a useful purpose, and he wearily thanks God for it. Yet when the storm passes him by, he rails against heaven: 'Je suis BOSSU! [...] Vous croyez que c'est facile?' (239). Jean's deformity is the primordial injustice of which he is the victim. But both God and nature continue to pursue him without mercy and he reacts violently against the 'iniquity' of their 'incompréhensible trahison' (239).

But Jean, the constitutional optimist, quickly comes to regard the continuing drought and the cruel sirocco as merely temporary setbacks and does not persist in blaming anyone but himself: 'Je pourrais accuser l'injustice du Ciel, ou des conditions atmosphériques exceptionnelles; je préfère attribuer mon échec à ma propre sottise, à mon manque de bon sens' (256). But he stubbornly persists in counting on his own efforts. Dowsing for water, a solution which lies half way between his belief in science and his faith in Providence, is merely one more hare-brained scheme. After recovering from his sunstroke, he is calm and resigned but no wiser, and soon he has mortgaged his property so that he can continue on the path to self-destruction. Papet's verdict on him seems all too well founded: 'c'est un homme qui n'a guère de chance' (278). Yet congenital optimism and temperamental impatience are the immediate cause of his death, for his destiny is as much written in his genes as in his stars. He can no more help the way he is than he can control the weather or defend himself against the Papet-Ugolin conspiracy, of which he is ignorant: as Milly had said in Fabien : 'On ne peut rien contre sa nature'. He stands convicted of pride, obstinacy and a lack of common sense, moral failings which might have responded to self-discipline. One of nature's innocents he might be, and worthy of our sympathy because we can see how persistently God, nature and men conspire against him. Yet Jean is also the victim of his own character.

2. Ugolin

Ugolin is twenty-four at the start of *Jean de Florette*, and has just finished his period of military service. Although old enough to have done so, he appears not to have fought in the Great War. His peacetime posting to Antibes widened his horizons and awakened his ambitions, and he returns with a perfectly sensible and commendably practical plan with which to make his fortune. His parents are dead and his only surviving relative is his uncle César, who insists on reminding him that he is not only the last of the Soubeyrans but the last of a 'famille de pendus'. Not surprisingly, perhaps, Ugolin, who is unadventurous, unassertive and a mild man of solitary tendencies, is not attracted by the idea of marriage and family duty. He is much more interested in money, and his friend Attilio has shown him how to make it. After a life of profitable toil, he hopes to retire in comfort 'dans son petit mas des collines où il pouvait parler tout seul à son aise, et compter—toutes portes fermées—ses pièces d'or' (J, 19). Ugolin's dream of a self-sufficient, peaceful country life is not really very different from the grander goals of Jean de Florette.

But whereas the forces which act on Jean originate as much in his own self-indulgence as in chance, nature and peasant covetousness, Ugolin is much more clearly the toy of external influences over which he has no control. His heredity will act against him; circumstances (his military service, for example, which gave him ideas without providing him with the means of achieving them) conspire to lead him into temptation; and love will make him mad before driving him to suicide. Not that Pagnol makes him particularly likeable. Ugolin's personal habits are appalling, he watches his gold coins grow with disturbing glee, and his moral sense runs a slow second to self-interest. When Papet suggests they return and finish off the unconscious Pique-Bouffigue, Ugolin is frightened and refuses, not because murder is wrong but because 'On nous a peut-être vus' (51). If he does a good turn for Jean, he hopes that God is watching (160). Yet, goaded by Papet, he lies and dissembles and plots ruin and disaster with the ease of a practised hypocrite. Ugolin, who was an innocent of sorts, turns into a victimiser.

And yet he is far from unsympathetic. Of course, he knows that by feigning to be a good neighbour he is helping the *bossu* to dig a pit for him to fall into. Yet though Jean is the obstacle to his happiness, the 'bossu de la ville' is the only person who treats him with a measure of respect and human warmth. Ugolin responds positively: Jean becomes his friend, an eventuality unforeseen in Papet's plan. Papet prompts him to a selfish and unfeeling course of action. But Jean's hopes and the spectacle of his happy family begin to unsettle Ugolin's introverted, self-absorbed habits of mind. Knowledge that he has blocked the spring makes him uneasy, not simply because he might be found out or because God may punish him, but because his conscience troubles him: his new-found friendship with his surrogate family has given him moral sense enough to know that he has acted wickedly. On the surface, he remains wily, shrewd and determined. Yet Pagnol is at pains to stress that 'un obscur remords [...] le travaillait à son insu' (160; 254). When Jean asks him to estimate the value of his property, Ugolin suggests an unreasonably high figure and is genuinely dismayed when it becomes the basis for his friend's last madcap scheme to raise a mortgage (271-5). Jean's death affects him profoundly. 'Une étrange douleur serra ses côtes, et il trembla d'épouvante lorsque de grosses larmes sautèrent à ses yeux'. He tells himself that books killed Jean, who would not listen to good advice: '"Moi, j'ai la conscience tranquille". Mais il pleurait toujours, sans savoir pourquoi' (287). And when, against Papet's advice, he allows the women to remain at the farm, the reason he gives (that they will be useful—293) does not deceive anyone: 'A sa propre surprise, il avait prononcé ces paroles avec une véritable émotion, et des larmes lui montèrent aux yeux' (299). If Ugolin is never the 'saint' that Aimée at first sees in him, neither is he the 'crapaud' that Manon believes him to be.

But the friendship which has watered his parched soul does not have lasting effects. For a while after Jean's death, he continues to feel pangs of conscience and 'pour obtenir pardon de ce crime, il offrit vingt petits cierges à saint Dominique'. But 'il était trop passionné par son entreprise pour s'attendrir durablement' (**M**, 8). His obsession is as a much a passion as that of, say, Phèdre. 'Tout entier à sa passion', he resumes his

lonely existence, 'sa pensée toujours occupée et comme
distendue par le présent' (13; 14). His sense of responsibility for
Aimée and Manon fades, and if time passes without his
noticing he explains that 'c'est la faute des œillets!' (41). He
tells himself that he has succeeded where Jean had failed, and
with success comes complacency: 'Enfin, chacun sa chance,
chacun son étoile. Les affaires des autres, ça ne me regarde pas'
(53). He makes money, amasses his gold and hides it where no
burglar will find it: 'malin, ça veut dire Ugolin!' (52). But
success fails to satisfy him. Within three years, he so prospers
that he no longer has to work. In a rare philosophical moment,
he stands back and considers his life: 'La vérité, c'est que plus
on en a, plus on en veut, et finalement, au cimetière. Alors, à
quoi ça sert?' (56). Yet it is his compulsive greed which leads to
his downfall. Had he uprooted his ageing carnations as M.
Trémélat suggested, he would not have seen Manon bathing in
her mountain pool....
    Pagnol, though, makes it clear that he has no choice in the
matter. He senses that in some strange way, Manon 'l'avait
attiré'. As he watches her, he feels the 'mystère d'une peur
émerveillée' and senses that she is 'la divinité des collines, de la
pinède et du printemps'. She fills him with 'une peur
inexplicable', 'une terreur sacrée' and 'une sombre folie
commençait à monter en lui' (64; 63; 61). He continues to tend
his flowers, but in that moment of bewitchment Manon has
replaced gold as his obsession. He realises that life is pointless,
since life always ends in death, yet human desire is relentless:
'Finalement, on n'est jamais content de rien' (72). But he
dreams of Manon, collects relics which he keeps in a 'sacred'
place and turns her into an object of adoration: she becomes 'la
Sainte Vierge sauvage' (98). She is clearly no Christian symbol
but the focal point of Ugolin's pagan superstitions. By the time
he performs his 'cérémonie magique' (127-8), it is clear that 'le
pauvre Ugolin des Soubeyran était en train de devenir fou'.
Heredity and fate have caught up with him. Ugolin, who
hounded Jean to death, has become the target of forces which
he does not understand and cannot fight. He accepts his ruin:
'C'est bien fait, je l'ai mérité' (163), though his financial losses
cease to matter to him. His plans no longer have any meaning
even as he defends them in public in Manon's presence:

'Oubliant les œillets et la source, il la regardait' (190). His suicide note makes it clear that he dies of despair and not because he fears the law or because his flowers are doomed. What was in his stars and in his heredity was not love, but madness and death. Alone with his body, Papet takes the festering love talisman and burns it 'dans la flamme purificatrice' (239). Ugolin, by turns innocent, victimiser and victim, is finally absolved.

3. Manon

Although she is given a pivotal role to play, Manon is the least complex of the major characters. She is too young in *Jean de Florette* to influence the course of events, though the first volume firmly establishes her uncritical adoration of her father and her intuitive dislike of Ugolin. By the time she is fifteen, she is aware that she is pretty (though less so than in the film, where she deliberately toys with men). In one of the rare moments when she resembles Prévost's *Manon Lescaut*, after whom, by way of several operas, she is named, Pagnol carefully notes that she is 'fière des compliments de ces hommes, et elle en riait de plaisir' (M, 20). She knows and loves the hills and though she reads anything from *Robinson Crusoe* to comics via the *Maximes* of La Rochefoucauld (22), she despises city culture. She is not really a tomboy, however, though at first she seems very young and idealistic: she dreams of marrying a rich man who will finish the well, find water and vindicate her father. She is self-contained, but her closeness to nature and to Baptistine makes her superstitious. The 'aversion irraisonnée' which she had felt for Ugolin changed into hatred the moment he became the owner of Les Romarins. Yet even after Ugolin declares his love she is puzzled by her revulsion, since Ugolin had gone out of his way to help her father. She tries to be fair: 'Peut-être vous n'avez rien fait de mal, mais je crois que vos services nous portent malheur: alors, ne vous occupez pas de nous' (121). Manon has difficulty in reconciling her natural feelings, which she trusts, with her memories of the past, which are vivid, and she is torn between her instinct and a sense of justice. As long as she exists in this state of moral uncertainty she remains the innocent, untamed creature who, occasionally observed by the villagers, acquires a supernatural aura. They regard her as a wild mountain girl, and Pamphile reports that he has seen her outrun a storm, 'comme un oiseau doré' (43). Even as a little girl she exuded an aura of magic and, as though she had stepped down out of a Greek fresco, 'parfois, sur des airs joyeux et saccadés, la fillette, les bras levés en amphore au-dessus de la tête, dansait pieds nus, sur l'herbe du printemps' (J, 165). Ugolin watches her communing with the *limbert* and concludes that she is a 'sorcière': 'Mais un jour il murmura, en riant de plaisir: "Quand une sorcière est belle, eh bien, ça s'appelle une fée!"' (M, 88).

Manon is thus a semi-mythological figure long before she overhears Pamphile and Cabridan reveal Ugolin's part in her father's downfall. Only then does she turn into an avenging fury, the instrument of dark forces. Her uncertainty vanishes and is replaced by rage. Her first thought is to shoot Ugolin, and the second to set fire to his farm. But nature first conspires against her before leading her to the grotto and handing her the means of punishing the whole village. It is at this point that Manon loses her purity and becomes an agent of destruction.

Bernard is quite right to see her as 'une nature fière, assez proche des bêtes sauvages, qui agit tout naïvement, et sans arrière-pensée' (239). To a certain degree, her search for retribution is natural and justified by the harm done to her and her family. But he also sees that she runs the danger of confusing justice with revenge. Even after Ugolin's death, she feels only repulsion and a grim satisfaction that he has been punished. Yet bitterness has not entirely destroyed her moral sense, and Bernard is able to persuade her to end the feud (250-2) and thus rescues her from the weight of guilt which the curé also sees hanging over her head. But Manon is not persuaded merely because her moral sense has survived her tribulations. Bernard has a special power over her. At first, she believes superstitiously that he is a threat because he has made her enter his dream, and it is through another dream that she realises that she truly loves him (83; 249). Pagnol makes her feelings quite explicit. When they go to unblock the spring, she pulls him through the narrow entrance of the grotto and 'pensait à la naissance d'un chevreau' (253). It is an unusually direct image which reveals that the attention she pays to his 'muscles de mâle' (and he to 'l'odeur tendre et sauvage de la fille des sources'—254) is as sexual as it is poetic. But Bernard has another power over her, for she readily identifies him with her father. 'Papa était chercheur d'eau, celui-là est chercheur d'or', she thinks when she sees him for the first time (35-6). He has eyes 'couleur de café brûlé, comme ceux de son père' (255) and in her dream, Bernard too has a *bosse*. He even thinks like her father when persuading her to undo the evil she has done and she confesses that he would not have succeeded 'si vous ne m'aviez pas parlé de mon père' (255). Bernard therefore brings her not only love, but becomes a father figure who fills the void left by Jean.

The effect on her is remarkable, for she is domesticated in the way a wild horse is broken. When she learns that Ugolin will receive a Christian burial, she says: 'Tant mieux pour lui!' (260), for now that love has ousted hatred she becomes strangely indifferent. The happiness she finds as a fully integrated member of the social order tames her completely, robs her of her mystery and turns her into a gentle creature of hearth and home. Bernard, who shares the local low view of women, increasingly takes control of her life. When Victor arrives with stories of the career Aimée might have had, Manon 'sentit obscurément que cette femme s'était sacrifiée à son mari' (281). But she is content to subordinate her own freedom to her future husband. In Bernard's view, Manon 'a une mentalité primitive, un esprit d'oiseau qu'on veut mettre en cage' (283), and this is exactly where he puts her. Manon, the wild mountain girl, becomes a submissive wife and mother. Although Pagnol clearly intended marriage as a happy ending for her, Manon, who began a victim and became a victimiser ends up as the victim of the patriarchal social order.

4. Le Papet

Jean, Ugolin and Manon seek to impose their desires upon their lives which they have every reason to expect will be long. Papet is sixty in 1922 and, by village standards, wants for nothing. He lives in the grandest house, is comfortably off and enjoys a position of respect. Philoxène may be mayor, but Papet exercises a kind of tribal authority. He is intelligent and he is experienced in the ways of the world and of the country: he is the first to see through the scientific jargon of the water engineer. But he is mean and sharp-tongued and is as suspicious of others as others are of him. He is envied and feared and prefers it so. Papet is self-contained and content to enjoy the mixture of respect and mistrust which he has cultivated.

Yet he has a secret regret. He has lived long enough to see his once great clan dwindle almost to nothing, 'car le malheur avait dévasté la famille' (J, 17). The wealth built up by generations of toil and sweat stands in danger of being left without a master, orphaned, annexed by unworthy hands. Peasant miserliness is certainly part of his sorrow. But Papet is César Soubeyran: he is named after an emperor and there is in Soubeyran (cf. Provençal *soubeiran*, sovereign) an unmistakable echo of *souverain*. He has a sense of dynasty which confers royal responsibilities upon him. If Lear divided his kingdom among his three daughters, Papet has no choice of heirs. Ugolin is the last of the line, the weak, twitching victim of the policy of inbreeding unwisely practised 'cousin-cousine, cousine-cousin' by 'les vieux' to keep the Soubeyran treasure in the family (M, 67). But if Papet's concern for the succession make him seem like an unhappy king who might have stepped out of ancient history or classical mythology, his sense of duty is also sacerdotal: he is chief priest, too, and he invests his mission with a sense of religious duty. Thus even Papet, who appears strong, decisive and self-contained, proves to be driven by an obsession.

But though a concern for family fortunes is in itself natural and even commendable, Papet defends his cause with ruthless single-mindedness. He is a violent man and turns mercilessly on Pique-Bouffigue for taking the Soubeyran name in vain. He is unforgiving towards Florette, who inherits Les Romarins, and he treats Jean without mercy. If he seems to go out of his way to avoid pushing Ugolin too hard, it is only because he has decided that patience is the best policy to adopt with his stubborn, slow-witted nephew. Although he initiates action, Papet's role is passive. He watches, guides and advises. He

puts ideas into Ugolin's head, comments on events with
confidence (as he predicted, Jean complains about 'routine'—J,
119; 138) and he stiffens Ugolin's resolve when Ugolin is in
danger of turning into a genuinely good neighbour (219-20). He
prods and prompts from the sidelines of the story, directing
events but also commenting on them like some baleful Greek
chorus. He repeats rhymes about the weather as though they
are magic incantations, and is always ready with superstitious
warnings ('il faut pas faire confiance aux bossus'—J, 118). After
Ugolin's suicide, he is on hand to perform rites which constitute
a form of pagan absolution (M, 239). Papet is a subtly-drawn
character of flesh and blood. But he is also a channel through
which mysterious forces move to destroy human happiness.

Like the rest of the villagers he is of course conscious of
these forces, but his own conduct is commanded by a much
more practical philosophy of action. Along with Jean, Ugolin
and Manon, he believes that ambitions can be achieved
through planning and effort. He pursues his dream—to restore
the family to greatness—according to a rational philosophy of
self-help. To Ugolin, who believes that the Soubeyran cause is
doomed, he replies angrily: 'Le Destin, ça n'existe pas! C'est
ceux qui ne sont bons à rien qui parlent du Destin! On a
toujours ce qu'on mérite' (M, 67). Papet seeks to impose his will
on reality by relying on cunning and determination. He
manipulates other people, deals cannily with lawyers' papers
and plans Ugolin's strategy for him: it is he, for example, who
thinks of blocking the spring. Papet, then, is not only a channel
through which stronger forces work: he is an *éminence grise*
strictly of this earth, who shapes the destinies of other people.

But for all his manoeuvrings Papet is doomed to fail, for he
in turn is helpless to resist the forces which he unwittingly
serves. After the death of Ugolin, he is left to survey the ruin of
the Soubeyran fortunes, the sole survivor of a royal clan. 'Eh
oui, c'est ça les Soubeyran... Trois fous, trois pendus, et moi
tout seul avec une jambe fadade... Et personne après moi...'
(240). But even then the gods have not finished with him, for
they send a messenger to set the seal on his misfortunes.
Delphine is blind, frightens children and speaks as through an
oracle which is as 'Delphic' as her name suggests. She is a
living statue—her expressionless face is 'un masque dur et

blanc comme du marbre' (295)—and through her is heard the laughter of the gods. Because Florette's letter never reached him the course of Papet's life was dislocated, and all his scheming to protect the dynasty had been worse than futile. For Jean was his son, a Soubeyran, and in persecuting him he had achieved the opposite of what he had intended. Papet, the destroyer of innocence, is as much a victim of the gods as Œdipus, the King of Thebes, whose fate is used by the curé as an awful warning. Ugolin's suicide note blamed no human agency and absolved even Manon from blame: 'c'est pas de sa fote, c'est pas de ma fote, c'est pas de ta fote c'est la fatalité' (239). Such is also Papet's conclusion: 'c'est la faute de l'Afrique' (312).

But if Ugolin could not be saved, Pagnol rescues Papet at the last moment by a final twist of fate. Manon's son is born early on Christmas Day at the same time as the old man's soul departs this life. It is a heavy piece of symbolism which seems to bring the drama under the wing of Christian providence, but is really another reminder of the existence of an older, tribal paganism. César de Soubeyran is dead; long live the Soubeyrans! The line is saved, even strengthened: had Ugolin married Manon, his niece, the breed would have been further weakened by another intermarriage. Papet dies without knowing that the gods have relented, but the reader is left with the assurance that Papet's sins have been forgiven and that life has come full circle. Through disaster, Papet has earned pardon. And in a way that he surely did not expect, he too has been given what he deserved.

*****

Jean, Ugolin, Manon and Papet thus illustrate Bernard's contention that 'les victimes ne sont jamais tout à fait innocentes' (M, 251), an idea which not only explains the shifts in emphasis as Pagnol focuses on the characters in their alternative guises but also constitutes the basic dialectic of the whole novel. For they are not the only ambiguous 'innocents' in L'Eau des collines. Pique-Bouffigue succumbs to the violence which he invited. Siméon, the poaching intruder whom he shoots, is also guilty of provoking the reaction from which he suffers. The stranger in the *curé*'s sermon who buys the house which collapses about his ears would not have died had he not fallen prey to *la folie des grandeurs* (M, 200). Indeed, the whole village becomes Manon's victim to the point where it almost dies: but the villagers are scarcely blameless, for even victims have an obligation to show charity and forgiveness (226). Their faults are moral and include pride, greed and indifference to others, but Pagnol's protagonists are guilty of having dreams of self-fulfilment which are not legitimate because they are obsessional, unhealthy and harmful to others. When thwarted, such passions are dangerous and are not to be tolerated. Racine remarked that Phèdre 'n'est ni tout à fait innocente ni tout à fait coupable'. As much must be said of Pagnol's cast of characters. And if Racine's heroine is pursued by Venus, so there are in *L'Eau des collines*, for all its substantial realism, forces at work which are equally mysterious. Jean is a 'bossu diabolique' and 'un magicien maléfique' (J, 154; 136), Ugolin is 'le paysan du Diable' (87), Manon a mountain nymph, and Papet is a royal chieftain who incurs the wrath of the gods. They are by turns the agents and targets of powers bent on erasing the fleeting joys of human existence and replacing them with 'd'inoubliables chagrins' (*supra*, p. 17). They are subject to the vagaries of an authority which rides roughshod over human will. Forces of unreason work through and against them, and none escapes unscathed from the inevitable cycle of fortune and misfortune.

Chapter Five

Pagnol and the Fates

The forces which weigh upon the characters of *L'Eau des collines* are not clearly labelled. But their presence is tangible in the way they shape events and in the way their victims attempt to make sense of their lives. The characters readily acknowledge their dependence on the natural world, and on the weather in particular. They also speak of Providence and destiny. Yet they are tempted to deny the existence of both Christian and pagan powers by interpreting events according to non-metaphysical and strictly humanist principles: they explain their misfortunes in rational terms and attribute them to personal faults, defective planning or sheer bad luck. The reader, of course, observes that events are directed by something greater than either the failure of human will to impose itself upon existence or the operation of some mechanical principle which punishes transgressors. But Pagnol does not offer us a single reading of these forces which favour some but harry others to despair and death. Instead, he offers a number of suggestions.

Christian Providence looms large, especially in *Jean de Florette*. On rare occasions, it is ironically invoked by the narrator. Thus when Ugolin's hopes are dashed by Pique-Bouffigue's refusal to sell Les Romarins, we learn that 'la Providence vint à son aide' (J, 62), for the old man dies conveniently. Yet 'providential' though Pique-Bouffigue's death may appear to be, this moment sets Ugolin on the road to perdition. Such authorial judgments are, however, rare and, for the most part, it is left to the characters to speak of heavenly intervention. From the start, Jean, who is an intermittently practising churchgoer, thanks God in word rather than in thought and deed. He asks heaven to bless his work and keep him strong and healthy, and he enthusiastically promotes Ugolin, whose arrival is 'la réponse du ciel', to the 'rang d'instrument de la Providence' (159; 160). But he does not

have a proper understanding of Providence, which is the word
given to the operation of God's goodness in ways which may
not always be understood by human minds. Whenever Jean's
plans succeed, he exclaims: 'Il est visible que la Providence a
décidé de récompenser nos efforts' (211). But when it refuses to
give him the rain he needs, he seeks reassurance not in prayer
but in weather statistics. For he has a greater sense of God's
obligation to be just than of His goodness (215). When the
storm saves him, he does not give thanks for 'un cadeau que
nous fait le Ciel' but defines it as an effect of 'le temps normal
de la saison'—although an afterthought suggests that 'cette
eau bénie' was well overdue and that Providence owed him a
helping hand (237-8). In other words, Jean is presumptuous and
views God as a kind of judge who punishes the wicked and
rewards the good. He may kneel in thanks when it rains after
his recovery from sunstroke (250), but as he begins to dig his
well, he remarks with the same naïve confidence in God the
Just: 'j'espère que la Providence ne me refusera pas cette
récompense' (257). The God who unfairly made him a *bossu*
owes him a great debt, and Jean's faith is easily shaken by any
instance of what he regards as divine injustice. In a moment of
'revolt', he even bellows heavenward: 'IL N'Y A PERSONNE
LÀ-HAUT?' (239). On the evidence, Jean has nothing to hope
for from the God he has made in his own image.

  Not surprisingly, Manon inherits her father's moralistic
view of Providence, which she too equates with a form of
natural justice. She regards Ugolin's success in finding a spring
as 'le comble de l'injustice' for he had obtained 'de la
Providence l'eau jaillissante qu'elle avait cruellement refusée
au meilleur des hommes' (M, 79). 'Sûre de son bon droit', she
believes that 'c'était sans aucun doute la Providence qui lui
avait révélé le secret de la source' in the grotto (161). When the
water in the bassin de la Perdrix turns red, 'elle sut que la
Providence lui accordait la ruine d'Ugolin, et la punition du
village' (145). Furthermore, if Ugolin loves her to distraction,
'elle pensait que Dieu lui avait envoyé cette passion
extravagante pour le punir de son crime' (247). As the villagers'
crops wilt, she feels that her father is vindicated: 'la brûlante
sécheresse qui allait compléter le désastre prouvait la
complicité de la Providence' (241). She even challenges God to

judge her actions. For though she does her part by unblocking
the spring in the grotto, no one can be sure that the water will
ever flow again. If it has found some other permanent channel,
'ce sera le signe que le Bon Dieu me donne raison' (260). But the
water does return and, in Manon's own terms, God has
weighed her thirst for vengeance and found it wanting.

Both Jean and Manon thus annex Providence and turn it
into a human principle of even-handedness and fair play,
rather as the *curé*, for all his acceptance of the mysterious ways
of heaven, is inclined to do: God is not Love, his sermon
concludes, but Justice. God's verdicts are as impenetrable as
they are surprising, and the only useful defence is repentance
and the practice of charity. Ugolin, on the other hand, does not
speak of Providence, an abstract, intellectual concept which is
beyond him, though his frequent invocations of 'le Bon Dieu'
spring from a not dissimilar set of assumptions. His God is a
stern, unloving force, both the brutal landlord of creation and
His own gamekeeper. When Ugolin plants weeds all over Les
Romarins, he does the 'Devil's work' which God,
incomprehensibly, protects (J, 87). For when he sees how the
brambles and thistles have flourished 'il médita [...] sur
l'extravagante vigueur des plantes inutiles, et le peu de santé
de celles qui rapportent de l'argent. Vraiment, le Bon Dieu
avait voulu nous forcer à travailler' (95). Unlike Jean, whose
sense of the beauty of nature leads him to admire God's
handiwork, Ugolin has only a sense of agriculture: his God is
judged by the way He helps (and more often hinders) human
efforts to scratch a living. His reaction explains why the other
'devil seeds' he sows in his campaign of lies and hypocrisy
against Jean will be justified by his utilitarian view of the
world, where only the fit and the cunning survive. But he also
has a healthy respect for God the all-seeing policeman. God
sends Jean rain to compensate for the spring which Ugolin
stopped: he senses that 'le Bon Dieu est contre nous' (210; cf.
192). As we have seen, Ugolin's conscience, a mixture of
genuine affection for Jean and peasant superstition, leads him
to an awareness of sin and the certainty that God (or at least
some terrible, omniscient, avenging power) will finally catch
him out and punish him.

God might well survey human actions from on high but He

is present in the story only in the distorted forms—as Judge and
Tyrant—which He takes in the minds of Jean, Manon and
Ugolin. A much more immediate shaping force, however,
surrounds them all the time. Though there are no dangerous
animals in the hills of Provence, life there is precarious. The
villagers are all vulnerable to the whims of nature. The very
survival of Les Bastides Blanches depends on its water supply,
and springs cannot be commanded even by science. The fertility
of the soil and the vagaries of the weather are part of a natural
order which does not give human beings a privileged place
above the plants and beasts on whom they depend. Life is
struggle and competition. Jean has a keen appreciation of
nature but he has also a practical understanding of the law of
the jungle. He tells Manon not to waste her sympathies on the
little birds she brings him: they may be pretty, but 'ce sont des
animaux féroces qui massacrent, pour les manger, de
minuscules créatures vivantes' (199). All of creation exists in a
state of competition, and all life is a battle.

Though the characters seek in their different ways to impose
their will upon existence, Pagnol consistently defines them as
part of the landscape by likening them to natural phenomena.
'Faisons comme les araignées', says Papet to Ugolin as he
outlines their plans (94-5). Jean recognises the misshapen
rowan tree as a 'confrère' in misfortune: it is 'ma statue en
bois', through which he survives death and becomes part of the
living landscape (M, 22). Manon is not simply 'la fille aux
sources' or the 'goat-girl' but is assimilated into her natural
surroundings. She has an 'épaisse crinière' (20), a 'soleil de
cheveux dorés' (308). She is alert and elusive as a fox (J, 198; M,
50), is likened to a grasshopper (53) and a jerboa (39; 43; 252).
She is nimble as a goat (61; 145) and swoops like a golden bird
(43). Ugolin's eyes twitch 'comme les étoiles' (J, 18), but from
timid and goat-like himself (18), he will be transformed into
'une bête puante' (M, 136), a scorpion (137), a wild boar (63).
Manon imagines his charred body 'tordu comme une vieille
souche d'olivier' (137), and when he dies he is pronounced
'raide comme un stoquefiche' (234).The village is an anthill (24),
and the Bastidiens are 'insectes' (134) who behave with 'une
férocité naturelle' (201). Éliacin herds the procession together
like 'un chien de berger' (266) and Enzo and Giacomo are

gigantic parrots (287). Adélie is as stubborn as 'un âne rouge' (J, 17), and she sweeps up 'moutons de poussière' (21) in Ugolin's house. Manon's anguished mind is 'désert comme la garrigue' (M, 134), an old soup-dish is as cracked as sun-baked clay in July (J, 103), and an argument flares up like fire in a barn (72). And if the Soubeyran clan is near extinction, one spark remains, like the glow which reignites a moorland fire, red like Ugolin's hair (M, 68). With such images, Pagnol merges his characters into the natural order which they cannot escape.

Another series of images describes natural phenomena in human terms and reveals nature in a variety of moods. When Jean appears, 'la pinède s'étonnait de voir passer un chapeau melon' (J, 181), birds too small to be shot know it and sing the louder (M, 55), and owls gather like old men 'sans doute à propos d'un sujet d'intérêt commun' (72). The jealousy displayed by the *limbert* towards Bernard is subjected to tongue-in-cheek psychoanalysis (294). When Manon sets out to free the spring, she walks through 'ce silence bleu de lune brodé de chants de grillons' (258). Nature wears 'écharpes de brume' (J, 238) and the branches of the olive tree 'caress' Jean's roof when the mistral blows (M, 137). There is hope that nature can be domesticated. With proper care, Papet's orchard could be 'beau comme une église' (J, 23); with a good water supply, the fertile earth of Les Romarins could grow 'des fraises comme des lanternes, des coucourdes comme des roues de charrette'. 'Tout ça,' says Ugolin, 'c'est plein de pièces d'or qui ne demandent qu'à pousser' (161).

Yet these visions of nature domesticated lie in the future. The present is harsh: the earth is hard as starch and the sun, 'un ballon de feu', 'va boire la moitié du vin' and 'discourages' Éliacin's aubergines (M, 186): in the night sky above Jean's head, the stars are cruel and dawn remains silent (J, 236-7). For nature is not always friendly and picturesque. Here are 'des pruniers hérissés de branches mortes maigres et noires, ou quelque antique figuier suffoqué par ses rejetons' (170), and Pamphile, who has cut down many trees, feels so oppressed 'que quand j'en vois des vivants, j'ose pas trop les regarder!' (M, 42). Springs are as 'perfidious' and faithless as a pretty girl. Even the village fountain which has sung for fifty years, 'respire', 'éternue', and dies. When Jean's maize withers, the

leaves look like parchment: they have reverted, it could almost
be said, to the paper on which he wrote his plans to grow them
(J, 250). Nature does not allow herself to be mastered without a
fight, and a further series of hostile images personifies natural
phenomena. There is a real sense that nature is a living thing
with a will of its own, moods which are frightening and a
never-sleeping antagonism to human desires. Flowers drink
'comme un homme' and the wooden stakes in Ugolin's fence
lean drunkenly, as though acknowledging that 'la terre avait
mangé leur pied' (31). When Manon sets fire to Les Romarins,
she imagines how 'les grands pins se tordraient les bras' in
their 'danse rouge' (M, 137). Yet nature is not so easily bent to
human will. Her plan is ruined by the storm which breaks
immediately: 'La pluie, qui avait si longuement trahi son père,
venait au secours de l'assassin' (139). This sense of nature's
awesome power is also conveyed in similes and metaphors
which maximise violence and terror. The wedge of Saint-
Esprit is like a reef against which the wind breaks 'comme un
fleuve' (J, 238); fire runs faster than horses and sends out sparks
like comets' tails (M, 139). Beautiful though the Provençal
landscape may be, it is also a place of violence and savagery
where drought and storm spare no creature. Nature, more
baleful bully than clumsy giant, can snuff out the lives and
dreams of the puny creatures which live in her shadow. Her
laws are unwritten but they are to be respected and feared: no
appeal is possible.

It is hardly surprising, then, if by extension all existence
seems to be controlled by mysterious force of fate. The death of
Giuseppe, on whose help Jean had counted, is 'l'arrêt du
Destin', and the sirocco which follows is another 'coup de pied
de l'âne du Destin!' (J, 230; 244). In his delirium, Jean insults 'le
Destin, la Providence, et le Sahara' (245), thus cursing the
pagan, divine and natural forces which are massed against
him. But Ugolin has an even deeper sense of doom. As he
watches Jean dig his well, 'il eut la certitude que cet homme
allait mourir': Jean's destiny was to live in a town and not try
to become a peasant (271-2). Ugolin tells dead 'Monsieur Jean'
that it was all his fault for having ideas, especially the
unworkable plan for raising rabbits; that the mountain was to
blame, or the books he had read (M, 73-4). But this attempt to

rationalise soon disappears beneath Ugolin's consciousness of
the irresistible forces which direct lives. He is drawn to Manon
by a fatal attraction, and if the Soubeyran line ends with him,
'ce n'est pas de ma faute! C'est le Destin!' (67). His final word,
in his suicide letter, accepts that no person is to blame: 'c'est la
fatalité' (239).

   This is an idea which deeply offends Papet's belief in his own
ability to shape events. He might talk perfunctorily of Jean's
'star' (J, 288) and concede that he was unlucky (278). But he is
much readier to lay the blame for Jean's failure on his ambition
and his book-learning (201; 288), thus interpreting events with
an earthly shrug rather than with a nod in the direction of the
supernatural. And if the Soubeyran line is dying, he angrily
rejects Ugolin's fatalistic explanation: there is no such thing as
Destiny, which is the excuse of the weak. 'On a toujours ce
qu'on mérite... Ce qui est arrivé, c'est la faute des vieux' (M,
67). Nor will he admit that there is anything paranormal in
Ugolin's bizarre conduct: 'cette petite l'a rendu fou' (224).
Manon too is tempted to demystify the drama of her father's
life and death: 'Ce n'était pas contre les forces aveugles de la
nature, ou la cruauté du Destin qu'il s'était longtemps battu;
mais contre la ruse et l'hypocrisie des paysans stupides,
soutenus par le silence d'une coalition de misérables... Ce
n'était pas un héros vaincu, mais le pitoyable victime d'une
monstrueuse farce, un infirme qui avait usé ses forces pour
l'amusement de tout un village' (134). A similar view is adopted
by Bernard: if the villagers did not take to Jean, the blame must
be laid at the door of the Soubeyrans (251). The curé too, in
insisting that 'Les vrais miracles, c'est dans les âmes que Dieu
les fait' (271), does not exclude divine intervention, but remains
firmly on the side of common sense.

   Yet even if we add the role of the Soubeyran heredity
(another kind of determinism which drives Ugolin to madness
and suicide and injects Soubeyran intelligence and tenacity into
the actions of Jean and Manon), the common-sense view that
all is to be explained by psychology and the course of events
seems scarcely adequate. There is no escaping the feeling that
the human drama is complicated by supernatural agencies in
which the superstitious villagers are all too ready to believe.
The hostility of nature is real enough but there are other

irresistible forces which play with human lives. If some invoke
Providence and Destiny, Philoxène the anticlerical mayor
proclaims: 'Je suis le maire LAÏQUE de cette commune, et les
miracles ne me font pas peur'—though it is only too clear that
they do (M, 272). And the blustering mayor is not alone in
sensing that life is in the final analysis directed by an authority
which is more powerful than the rules and practices of the
visible world. If Manon relents, it is not only because her love
for Bernard and his assimilation into Jean have undermined
her anger, but because she too is finally brought to
acknowledge a wisdom which is non-human, timeless and
inescapable. Jean, says Bernard, is avenged: Ugolin is dead,
Papet is 'à demi fou de rage et de chagrin' (251), and the
villagers have lost half their crops. If Manon persists, what
will become of the women and the children? And what price
goodness? For did not Pamphile, who painted the arrows for
Jean, also pay for his coffin? Where shall her vengeance end?
He quotes the words of God of Israel which set a limit upon
retribution: '"S'il reste un seul juste dans cette ville, elle ne sera
pas détruite"' (M, 252). Who is that just man who will redeem
the village? Bernard's candidate is Pamphile and, in accepting
his argument, Manon also accepts that justice is incomplete if it
is not leavened by mercy. She is brought back from the brink by
a reminder of a law which transcends the human.

Papet, the unbeliever, is no less surely made to understand
that there is more to life than fixing goals and striving to reach
them. He placed his faith in his own will and his own efforts.
But Delphine's revelations show that life is not simply a human
drama, and accident or weakness of purpose are not enough to
explain the defeat of dreams. He had once claimed that he had
never married because 'ce n'était pas bien dans mon caractère',
just as it was not in Florette's to say that she loved him (M, 67;
300). But through Delphine he sees how little 'character' had to
do with the irony of things, and he is left with little choice but to
acknowledge the power of destiny. It was 'because of Africa'
that Florette's letter miscarried, that Jean was persecuted, that
Ugolin died, and that his own hopes turned to ashes. We are as
convinced as Papet that events are to be explained by more
than chance, and what best accounts for the mysteries is the
pagan glee of the gods of ancient mythology, who seem

perfectly at home in a novel where the principal characters, as we have seen, wear otherworldly, pagan masks and play the parts of magicians, devils, nymphs and ancient kings. It comes as no surprise, therefore, when we learn that the capricious gods, their thirst for human misery slaked, finally relent. Once Papet has made amends by his public confession of the truth in his letter to Manon, they end their persecution and allow the Soubeyran clan to continue.

But is Pamphile the only just man in the saga? According to another piece of Biblical wisdom, which Bernard does not quote but which seems apposite, 'there is not a just man upon earth, that doeth good, and sinneth not' (*Ecclesiastes*, vii: 20). If this is so, then the field widens to include even Ugolin, by way of Jean, Manon herself and Papet too. For in spite of their sins, they are all 'pure' after a fashion: if they are not 'just', they were, according to their lights, 'justified' in having their dreams. Papet, the curator of the Soubeyran inheritance, is not punished for what he wants but for wanting it so obsessively and for treating those who stand in his way without mercy. Even so, the continuation and cleansing of the line amount to a favourable judgment. It is as though Papet, for all his sins, is the one 'just' survivor who ensured that the dynasty would not be destroyed. And so the will of the gods is finally joined to the unbending wisdom of the Old Testament in a moment of general amnesty and absolution. The dead have paid the price for their sins and have redeemed the survivors, who, made wiser by experience, remain to carry the torch of human values.

*****

If Manon's son is born on Christmas Eve at precisely the same moment as Papet departs this life, it is through the concerted action of Christian Providence and pagan Destiny. The birth wipes the slate clean and offers a new start: the dreams and destinies of Jean, Ugolin, Manon and Papet have dwindled until they are concentrated in this new soul: it is a moment of truce between the past, which is complete, and the future, which is unknown.

But the appearance of the child is not merely a neat

structural device which enables Pagnol to condense his novel until it is contained at one focal point. It is also an outrageous coincidence which can only be explained by his concern for his characters. Jean and Ugolin were irretrievable and he allowed them to die. But at the last he intervenes to save Papet's honour, just as he had intervened to prevent Manon compounding her guilt with the sin of vindictiveness. Pagnol's affection for his characters is clear enough and his protectiveness towards them must count as one of the forces which shape their fate. But though we may judge this last intervention to be intrusive, it is well prepared.

Throughout the novel, the narrator adopts a view of people and events which is distinctly paternal. The villagers may be unpleasant and selfish, but their cruelty and insensitivity are consistently presented as childlike and, on occasion, downright childish. Philoxène is the leader of a playground gang of 'mécréants' which includes Ange, the *fontainier*, who is constantly fretting about his pipes, Monsieur Belloiseau, who is almost in his second childhood, and Pamphile, who is a little boy to his Amélie. For all his giant's strength, Éliacin at times seems hardly grown-up at all. Pagnol even extends the treatment to the ebullient, mischievous Monsieur Victor, who is 'un peu ridicule parce qu'il ne parlait que de lui—mais il avait de gros yeux noirs d'enfant' (M, 280). The faults of Victor are thus redeemed, for childlike qualities are a test of that purity which Pagnol prized so highly. In much the same way, the *curé*, who views the villagers as so many naughty children, nevertheless believes that they have souls and need to be rescued from their follies and vices. Pagnol, who stands over them all, proves to be no less fatherly, and he saves them, their way of life and their village because he was too fond of them to administer more than a sharp lesson in brotherly charity and civic duty.

His other characters, by turns victims and victimisers, are much more complex than the village 'extras', but they too are 'just' according to their lights. Their purity is equated with the spontaneous, thoughtless innocence of childhood. They are without exception children or at least childlike—even Papet, who does not live quite long enough to receive the Christmas present he had asked for. Jean is an overgrown schoolboy given to crazes. He claps his hands eagerly when the long-awaited rain begins to fall, and he is fascinated by the power of dynamite, 'comme le sont en général les enfants' (J, 238; 280). Ugolin is so keen to get on with his flower-growing that Jean's unexpected appearance on the scene makes him as ill as a spoilt child denied a toy, and impatience makes him grow thin. He thinks that blocking the spring is 'une bonne farce', as though it were some schoolboy prank, and his ritual designed to put burglars off the scent is a piece of childish superstition. Even his miserliness is made to seem like coin-collecting, and he duly asks Papet for the few he needs to complete his 'set' of five hundred. He seems to need a father figure, and both Papet and 'Monsieur Jean' fit the bill. Though Manon behaves with a sense of purpose beyond her years, she is another child, and part of Bernard's attraction for her is that he is a father substitute. She has all the self-absorption of children: 'Comme presque tous les enfants, elle ne savait à peu près rien de la vie passée de ses parents' (M, 280). At first, her innocence deadens the grief she feels at her father's death: 'la puissante joie de vivre de la jeunesse, dont la chair expulse si vite les corps étrangers, adoucit le contour des mauvais souvenirs, en obscurcit les cruelles couleurs, et finit par leur donner l'irréalité d'une histoire lue dans un livre' (122). But life contaminates her innocence with 'la "précieuse" expérience' just as it destroyed Marcel's in Pagnol's autobiography, where grizzly bears stepped back into the pages of his natural history book, never to re-emerge. L'Eau des collines, in its more oblique way, pursues the values of the Souvenirs d'enfance, for it identifies certain kinds of idealistic conduct with the purity of childhood and shows how few dreams survive in the world of adult realities. It is through childlike eyes that Jean glimpses his ideal of self-sufficient country living, that Ugolin imagines fields red with carnations and golden with money, that Manon perceives her goal as nothing less than total vengeance and the destruction of her enemies, and that Papet views his defence of Soubeyran honour.

Pagnol does not cast them as children to make them foolish, though, like Monsieur Victor, they are sometimes mildly ridiculous. On the day of their wedding, Manon and Bernard make a handsome couple, 'mais on voyait bien qu'ils le savaient, et qu'ils n'étaient pas modestes du tout' (M, 287). It is hardly a severe criticism of their pride, but a moment of tender complicity which enables bride and groom to keep their dignity and Pagnol to make a wry comment on their innocence. And when Bernard calls at the baker's after the birth of his son, 'on vit bien que c'était un prétexte, et qu'il venait pour recevoir des félicitations; il se montra aussi fier que s'il avait fait cet enfant tout seul: [...] et l'on voyait bien qu'il se félicitait lui-même d'avoir fait un enfant comme on n'en avait jamais vu' (306; 307). Joseph, in *La Gloire de mon père* (p. 305), had similarly toured the village, immodestly boasting of his hunting exploits and had been taken 'en flagrant délit d'humanité'; Bernard here is just as guilty and as leniently judged, for such self-satisfaction, unlike the obsessiveness of Jean or Ugolin, harms no-one. And so, far from demeaning them or exploiting their follies for comic purposes, and unwilling to allow life just yet to blight their dreams, Pagnol extends a protective hand to his brood.

What therefore seems like manipulation of events to produce a 'happy ending' is rather an expression of Pagnol's understanding of human weakness and compassion for life's victims, even the least deserving of them. When he intervenes, he ceases to be the ironic, detached chronicler of their acts of victimisation and he enters his story, sharing their griefs, allowing them moments of triumph when he can, but unable to prevent those who are beyond his help from meeting the fate to which their wilfulness has brought them. He permits them all to keep at least a measure of dignity, and in so doing he tempers the sterner judgments of nature, the gods and the Old Testament. Pagnol may be an indulgent father, but he is rarely sentimental. It is his resigned kindliness and gentle humour which prevent his tale from being a tragedy, and stamp his account of the perils of innocence with an irresistible, resilient human warmth.

Chapter Six

Structure, Style and Humour

Although the mood of *L'Eau des collines* is more austere than the openly comic 1952 film of *Manon des sources*, Pagnol stops well short of the tragic, nor does he express any hint of bitterness. He does not protest against the incoherence of the universe, the injustice of nature or man's inhumanity to man. On the contrary, he seems happy enough standing above the world he creates, intervening occasionally, but maintaining the viewpoint of a sympathetic, amused and only partly involved observer. He understands the despair of his characters but does not share it, though he clearly feels it enough to rejoice when dreams comes true and commiserate when plans go astray. Pagnol, the 'optimiste angoissé', adopts a stance of cheerful stoicism or, perhaps more accurately, of ironic fatalism which excludes all varieties of hand-wringing. He was not interested in abstract thought and never expounded a system of ideas. His doctrine, if such it be, derived from his resilient, buoyant and positive attitudes to life and was a matter of personality rather than of philosophy. His values were those of an old-fashioned republican conservative who believed in traditional family life, personal responsibility and hard work. He set great store by the notion of honourable behaviour enshrined in the notion of 'decency': integrity, concern for others and a sense of collective responsibility. But he was too much of an individualist to be a puritan, and was always prepared to sanction infringements of the code in those 'just' characters whose dreams and ambitions set them above the common herd which, on the whole, he rather despised. Indeed, his secondary characters tend to be caricatural representations of human folly and stupidity, though his tone is rarely censorious but affectionate. Even the most pompous, pretentious or insensitive are permitted to redeem themselves with touches of delicate feeling: Monsieur Victor may be foolish, but Pagnol stresses 'la tendresse de ce gros homme qui n'avait pas été célèbre pour rien' (M, 281).

Even so, Pagnol's attitude to his characters and his occasionally indulgent manipulations of the plot (which, for example, permit Aimée's future to be conveniently catered for by Monsieur Victor) reflect the principle of 'superiority' which he had identified, in an essay entitled *Notes sur le rire* (1947), as the essence of comedy. To appreciate a joke, the spectator must feel superior to the person on whom the joke is perpetrated. I am not amused when I slip on a banana skin, though I laugh if it happens to someone else. More than a restatement of Bergson's famous definition of comedy as 'du mécanique plaqué sur du vivant', Pagnol's argument stresses the active complicity of reader or spectator, who feel better-informed and more intelligent than the victim of the joke. The successful comic writer is therefore he who flatters his audience by giving them privileged information. Of course, comedy always distances the observer from the observed, and of necessity it dehumanises the object of the joke. Our laughter ceases the moment the victim becomes human: if the man who slips on the banana skin breaks his leg, his suffering brings him too close for us to remain detached. The comic author must therefore ensure that his characters remain in an 'inferior' position. Pagnol's gift for turning comedy into unexpected tragedy—and back again—depends on cunningly-arranged variations in the distance which separates us from the world he creates. Both the narrative stance and the confidential tone of voice of *L'Eau des collines* ensure that our view of people, places and events is that of the 'superior' observer. We see the drama unfold from above and laugh at the foolish villagers we meet. But there are moments when Pagnol removes the platform on which he has set us and we are brought unexpectedly close to unhappiness, blighted dreams and death. Pagnol's unique blend of humour and sadness derives from gentle and subtle manipulations of his reader. Just as his characters are pursued by fate, we too are playthings of Pagnol's literary artifice. By turns, we are both above and in the story, and our 'superiority' is at crucial moments so undermined that our detachment vanishes altogether and we are left with no alternative but to identify with the spectacle of human suffering.

Pagnol delights in wrong-footing his reader. Like some kindly uncle, he seems to take us fully into his confidence, and we watch his stories unfold over his shoulder from his point of view. And yet at moments, he springs surprises which jolt us out of our complacent acceptance of his urbane world view and force us to think—and feel—for ourselves. He introduces a circumstance which has gone unmentioned, perhaps, or he may show us an event, a reaction or a character in a new light. Most of his sudden changes of direction amount to no more than a warning against making hasty judgments, but others come with the force of a revelation which mobilises our emotions rather than simply our minds. He makes mild fun, for instance, of the excited blessings, comprehensible only to Giuseppe, which Baptistine showers on the Cadoret family. But two pages later the narrator tells us that we should not mock: this 'formule piémontaise' is so powerful that the Virgin Mary not only understands, but is 'incapable d'y résister' (J, 176; 178). Baptistine suddenly ceases to be a superstitious freak and acquires a kind of talismanic authority. The technique may sometimes reflect no more than the comic principle of the unexpected, as in the story of how Eliacin turned the tables on the army, and on us (M, 218). But more usually Pagnol makes the switch in order to destabilise our responses (rather as Dylan Thomas does in *Under Milk Wood* when he tells us that Bessie Bighead was once kissed by Gomer Owen when she was not looking, but never kissed her again 'though she was looking all the time'). The same deflation of the comic by a quick injection of wistfulness is found in the reasons why Baptistine and Giuseppe remained at Le Plantier. Giuseppe had told her they would stay 'jusqu'à ce que tu aies le premier mal au cœur' and then move to the village: 'ils y étaient restés toutes ces années parce que le mal au cœur du matin n'avait jamais voulu venir' (J, 174). The same mixture of humour and vulnerability recurs many times, in Ugolin's dramatic tirade in Bernard's garden, for example: Jean 'a vu sécher ses coucourdes, et ça fait pleurer tout le monde. Et moi, au même endroit, je vais voir crever mes œillets, et je vais mourir d'amour pour toi, et ça fera de la peine à personne' (M, 223).

But the contradictions and abrupt changes of mood create multiple ambiguities in broader matters. Pagnol's lyrical appreciation of nature seems to suggest that he sympathises with Jean's revulsion against 'l'enfer des villes' and the

VI: Structure, Style and Humour

contempt which the earthy Bastidiens have for townspeople. Yet he can also judge the villagers as harshly as the lawyer who asks for Pique-Bouffigue's head (J, 44-5). Moreover, he despises their mistrust of book-learning and counters the sentimental view which states that rustic ignorance is bliss: 'les travaux manuels (quoi qu'en disent les démagogues) n'exigent pas un véritable génie, et [...] il est bien plus difficile d'extraire une racine carrée qu'une racine de genêt' (J, 155). If Pagnol's own views are disguised and made ambivalent, we are also kept guessing by the shifts of emphasis which make it difficult to know where the centre of the novel is located. As the story unfolds, the stage is occupied in turns by Ugolin, Jean, Ugolin again, Manon and finally by Papet, so that we hesitate in identifying the real hero of the tale: not until the end do we suspect that perhaps the main character might be Papet, who has abetted plans of which he is the most tragic victim. Nor does Pagnol make it easy for us to adopt a settled view of the protagonists, who change and break out of the categories we assign to them: victims turn into victimisers and persecutors become innocents. More generally still, we are left wondering about the precise nature of the fictional universe of *L'Eau des collines*. It is filled with too many strange forces for it to be realistic; but it is too solidly anchored in reality to be magical.

Pagnol's exploitation of his reader is very clearly reflected in the overall structure of *L'Eau des collines*. The orderly introduction to the region, Les Bastides Blanches and its inhabitants establishes the narrative voice as omniscient and confidential and puts us in the author's pocket. Our position is privileged and 'superior', for we continue to be informed about matters kept hidden from the main characters. The first phase of the plot informs us fully of Ugolin's plans and actions, which we view from above and judge to be a mixture of innocent ambition and wickedness. The second phase, which centres upon Jean's struggle to impose his will on Les Romarins, exploits our 'superiority' for dramatic purposes. We know what Jean does not: the hidden motive behind Ugolin's neighbourliness and the existence of the blocked spring. We are thus enabled to appreciate to the full Ugolin's criminal behaviour, Jean's foolishness and the irony of the struggle between good and evil. But there is nothing in the affable, amused narrative tone to prepare us for Jean's death. We have been privileged witnesses to murder, of course—Pique-Bouffigue shot Siméon and was left for dead by Papet—but the deaths of these minor characters were not entirely unexpected elements in the picture of peasant life. Moreover, they were 'safe' murders from our point of view, for they are instances of violence perpetrated at a distance by actors within the drama. But when the stone falls on Jean's spine, our sense of shock is of a different order, for the violence is perpetrated on us. The narrator has played us false, disguised his intentions, laid a trap and misled us. Our 'superiority' and detachment vanish, for we suddenly know and understand no more than the survivors: we are plunged into a human tragedy which forces us to respond in kind. We no longer look down from a height, for we have become involved in the drama.

For the third phase, which starts at the beginning of the second volume, the narrator reverts to complete candour and once more makes us party to privileged information. Ugolin believes that he can win Manon, but we know that he never will. Our 'superior' knowledge enables us to savour the irony and pathos of his fate, and his death does not come as a surprise but emerges naturally from the inevitability of things. Phase four also gives us important information denied to all except Manon: we know she has blocked the spring in the grotto and this knowledge enables us to view with detachment the panic of the villagers, the impotence of the water engineer and the *curé*'s earnest sermon . Our confidence in the narrator reassures us that Manon will relent and that the village will be saved. And so it proves. But in the final phase, the narrator springs another surprise. There is nothing to prepare Delphine's revelation, and our special relationship with the author is again denied: we may appreciate the irony of the letter which miscarried, but we do so not 'from above' but on the ground, as fellow sufferers with Papet, whose life suddenly collapses around him. Of course, Pagnol does not leave us callously in ignorance. He lets us off the hook by taking us into his confidence once again at the end, just as he posthumously grants César's wish to see his line continue. But by dropping us into the story and abolishing the distance separating us from events, he ensures that we are both involved and detached, both in the story and above it. It is thus that we receive the full force of his pessimism: Pagnol's genial irony never strikes us more strongly than at this moment, as we step back to survey the ruins.

The most dramatic of these changes of direction are strategically placed. The first volume ends with Jean's death and Delphine's revelation closes the second. Both parts of the novel share the same structure. Part one focuses on two characters, Ugolin and Jean, with an endpiece showing Ugolin's triumph. Part two follows Ugolin and Manon, and adds a coda devoted to Papet, with whom the story began. And within each part, within each character, another structural principle—the dialectic of victim and victimiser—is at work. These architectural symmetries ensure that the drama is not merely unified but made intense, and the effect is to suggest that life is merely the orchestration of simple themes: water, which gives life, and dreams, on which our human happiness depends. The structure is undisturbed by the appearance of new characters (Bernard and the new *curé* most obviously), for they are are easily absorbed into the established progression of events. Yet at the same time, Pagnol also suggests that though things change, they do no necessarily move forward. The birth of Manon's son returns us to the beginning of the story. With Ugolin's suicide, Papet became the 'last of the line', and when he dies, the title is inherited by Manon's son and the wheel comes full circle. Nothing has been settled except the efforts of one generation. The story of life has no beginnings or endings: it is one long middle.

* * * * *

The careful symmetries and circular structure of *L'Eau des collines* give the clearest expression to Pagnol's fatalism. And though he might appear to be cruel at those moments when he suddenly withdraws our privileged status as 'superior' observers, his general tone and his handling of situation and character ensure that our awareness of tragic destiny is diluted by comedy. There is, to begin with, a vein of satirical observation. He lampoons townspeople who have an idyllic view of the country, but is not particularly anxious to defend

the peasantry: the inhabitants both of Les Bastides Blanches
and Crespin are 'pareillement jaloux, méfiants et secrets'. He
pours scorn on the peasant mistrust of education, but also
mocks 'intellectuals' (Jean, Bernard, the water engineer) who
believe that all questions are answered in books. He laughs at
Philoxène, who is mayor because he has a telephone, and the
curé, who is not above asking for a dozen eggs, or for his
drains to be unblocked, in the middle of a sermon (**M**, 199). But
the satire is invariably mild and is intended to hold up human
foolishness not to censure, but to gentle ridicule.

In the same way, Pagnol makes a sparing use of farce, a
comic technique which dehumanises and appeals to our sense
of cruelty. Indeed, apart from Amélie's throwing the stew out
of the window, Éliacin's ferocious demand for the water he has
paid for, Ugolin's efforts to make himself presentable, or the
effect Monsieur Belloiseau's collapsible top-hat has on the
village children, there is much less comedy of situation than in
the film, where all these incidents, together with Manon's
'trial', Belloiseau's exploding deaf-aid and his encomium to
Ernest Lacombe on the occasion of the village fête are
exploited to the full. To comedy of action, Pagnol prefers a
subtler comedy of character which reveals human folly in what
people do. Monsieur Trémélat's roundabout approach to
business, Monsieur Victor's extravagant behaviour, Amélie's
rages and even the robust presence of the *curé*, all create an
impression of generalised eccentricity. But if the novel is much
less a series of comic incidents than the film, and exploits a
more general comedy of situation, it is also far less rich in high-
profile comic characters. As we have seen, Pagnol discarded
the pompous police sergeant and demoted Monsieur
Belloiseau: neither is replaced, though Monsieur Victor, who
makes a brief appearance, is clearly their heir. The humour of
L'Eau des collines loses in terms of *le gros rire*, but it gains in
subtlety. As a film maker, Pagnol was obliged to translate
motive and psychology into incident and behaviour. As a
novelist, he discovered that, to a practised raconteur like
himself, telling a story meant primarily imposing a tone of
voice and adopting a certain level of mimicry. The need was
not, therefore, to invent more comic characters and incidents,
but to vary the dramatic pace of a slowly developing organic

situation and to direct the responses of the reader to the heart of the tale. The action is less important than the way it is shaped for our ears. *L'Eau des collines* is a novel of voices. Whenever the actors in Pagnol's tragicomedy fall silent, the narrator fills the silence with directorial comments. Pagnol's comic technique thus relies heavily on manipulations of language: with a word or phrase, he brings us to a stop or diverts us into a side road, like a policeman directing traffic. Our responses are conditioned by the interpretation he puts on events and people, and what the characters do is often less revealing than what they say, and certainly much less amusing than their extravagant way of saying it.

Or not saying it. Pagnol's fascination with language is clearly visible in the unusually large number of his characters who have speech problems of various kinds. Anglade's twins stutter and complete each other's sentences, while Papet's dumb servant communicates only in grunts. Baptistine's French is minimal and she needs Manon to interpret for her. In contrast, Attilio speaks three dialects, but though his French is 'convenable', he often uses 'deux adjectifs l'un sur l'autre' (M, 5). But those who have tongues more than make up for those who do not. They revel in picturesque turns of phrase, graphic metaphors and unexpected similes. Ugolin in his finery tells himself proudly: 'si je me rencontrais j'oserais pas me parler' (116). Philoxène, defending himself with a hammer, warns Éliacin that if he indeed intends to set fire to the town hall, he would be well advised to come armed with 'une allumette plus longue que le manche de ce maillet' (188). Victor describes one admirable soprano as 'un rossignol dans un baobab', while another, 'qui avait les dimensions d'une locomotive, en avait aussi le sifflet' (276; 277). Into the mouths of his characters, Pagnol puts the expressive 'parler savoureux' which most French people associate with the Midi. They give out wisdom couched in homely images: engineers, says the *curé*, 'sont des gens qui piochent tout le temps, et qui ne plantent que des pylônes' (196). They have a splendid line in exuberant invective: 'si les moulins à vent pouvaient parler', Papet says of Pamphile, 'ils diraient les mêmes choses que lui' (J, 292). Even their throwaway lines acquire the status of vivid and—literally—pungent aphorisms. Commenting on the

mule's 'asphyxiante pétarade', Papet remarks: 'Si cette bête
avait le nez à la place de la queue, elle ne pourrait plus vivre'
(29). Pagnol learnt early in his careeer to beware of 'la formule
à l'emporte-pièce', but happily for us found it difficult to resist
spicing his dialogue with such outrageous one-liners, which
maintain the comic mood and avoid any hint of mawkishness.

Such verbal extravagance is of course part of Pagnol's
careful effort to capture the linguistic realities of Lower
Provence. A few genuine Provençal expressions help in
creating this atmosphere: *'bessaï; Ven de nuei / Duro pas
ancuei; Sian pouli; porcas; cago ei braio; Faï de ben à
Bertrand, ti lou rendra en caguant!'* (M, 28; 149; 178; 208; 216).
But his peasants' imperfect grasp of French is also a rich source
of humour. He exploits their speech, with its grammatical
mistakes, mispronunciations and misunderstandings, for comic
purposes: Papet is no clearer than Ugolin about what Jean's
'cultiver l'authentique' means. Their ignorance appears very
clearly in the letters written by Attilio ('Ô Collègue! Tu te
dessides?'—J, 57), Graffignette (who is given to pious
platitudes), Ugolin ('Je vous écrit à vous pasque c'est du sérieut
de notère'—M, 235) and Papet ('cé mon reire petit-fils'—M,
311), and even the poignancy of last letters is sweetened by
their atrocious spelling. At times, Pagnol cannot resist more
open mockery, of Jean's earnest application when he
'commença (soyons méthodiques) par l'installation du potager'
(J, 163), say, or when he gives a straight-faced, reported
version in purple prose of Attilio's enthusiasm for his
floricultural calling which has been expressed with 'une poésie
véritable' but doubtless in some mixture of languages barely
recognisable as French: 'il s'attendrit sur la fragilité des
boutures, l'infinie richesse des coloris de l'œillet Malmaison...
Il fulmina contre l'araignée rouge, parla durement du pou du
Mexique, et critiqua le directeur de la criée d'Antibes qui
favorisait honteusement les Italiens' (M, 7). Pagnol derives
some of his best effects from such bravura passages which mix
pastiche and parody.

But if in similar vein Pagnol also mocks the scientific jargon
of the water engineer, he clearly has a weakness for characters
who use long words. Jean is a regular offender, but so is
Monsieur Belloiseau, who remarks that if Bernard approaches

Manon carefully, he might 'pousser très loin une petite idylle minéralogique, automnale et champêtre' (M, 238). But the narrator will not be outdone and, drowning out the authentic voice of Provence, yields to the temptation of lexical overkill. In his autobiography, Pagnol explains that he used to collect 'interesting' words (like *anticonstitutionnellement*) as other boys collected marbles: in the same spirit, he allows Monsieur Belloiseau to explain, quite gratuitously, the etymology of that interesting word 'scrupule' (M, 242-3). As a 'writer of prose', then, Pagnol occasionally allows his love of florid vocabulary to run riot. Polysyllabic words, their Graeco-Latin roots showing above ground, flourish like the bramble bush which 'étendait en rond d'ombrageantes branches richement feuillues' (J, 19) at the door of the 'mas de Massacan'. Sometimes the transferred epithets ('les tuiles amicales' which Ugolin brings, or Jean's 'gargouillantes espadrilles') aid in the personification of nature. At other times, they form part of extended descriptions which satirise in the most 'superior' way the 'glorieuse et commerciale litanie' of Saints' Days (M, 49) or the close of the *curé*'s sermon:

> Alors sous les doigts de Mme Clarisse, l'harmonium attaqua un psaume, et les voix aigrelettes et maigriottes des enfants de Marie s'élevèrent, humanisées par tant de sournoise innocence. Les voix suppliantes des vieilles les agrémentèrent aussitôt de trémolos involontaires dont le timbre cristallin révélait l'absence d'hormones et la crainte inexplicable de la bienfaisante mort. Alors le baryton de M. le curé, un peu épais, mais cartésien, remit de l'ordre dans la divagante mélodie, puissamment soutenu par les mugissements liturgiques d'Éliacin. (M, 204)

Here, Pagnol chooses as many of the longest and most flowery nouns, adjectives and verbs as his phrases will bear. He prefers the more resonant diminutive form whenever possible (*aigrelettes, maigriottes*) and, for greater emphasis, puts adjectives before the nouns they qualify (*divagante mélodie*). The combinations are unexpected (*trémolos involontaires*) and even paradoxical (*sournoise innocence; bienfaisante mort*). The long sentences with their elegant sub-clauses and tripartite structure (the voices of children, women and men) move inexorably forward according to the rules and rhythms of classical rhetoric. It is comic because it is incongruous: the inappropriately ornate style makes the cacophony even more absurd than it is in reality.

Pagnol directs our responses and comes between us and what he shows us, and what he shows us is magnified and enhanced. An eagle becomes a 'tournoyant agresseur' (M, 35), we see 'les voletantes étincelles des lucioles' (J, 214), and we hear 'l'hérétique angélus des tintinnabulantes casseroles' on the day Ugolin becomes 'le Roi des Œillets' (J, 312). Sometimes the technique expresses Pagnol's wistful affection for his characters: we know Ugolin is many things, but as a 'fleuriste désespéré' (M, 245) he is both absurd and touching. Lushness of language thus becomes a comic technique, and its mockery is tempered by affection. Ugolin's moustache 'avait été sacrifiée, mais au profit de son nez qui paraissait deux fois plus long' (115). If the humour here hangs as much on the ironical use of *au profit de* (the advantage is gained not by Ugolin but by his regrettable nose, so that the whole venture is made pointless), elsewhere Pagnol gives the verb *faire* three different objects in informing us that Célestine, the *curé*'s *bonne à tout faire*, 'faisait tout en effet, même le désespoir de M. le curé, et la joie des garçons du village' (30). By applying sophisticated, rotund and generally inappropriate linguistic registers to subjects which will not bear their weight, Pagnol distances us from what he shows us and determines our responses. His sophisticated use of language is thus not merely a rich source of comedy but a reminder of who is in charge of the story.

Pagnol does not refrain from using the authority of the narrator to pass judgment, usually in the form of maxims, upon people and events. His pithy comments do not always express quite the same angle of vision, and the perspective is doubled and tripled. He can judge compulsive behaviour sharply: 'C'est un fait que les imbéciles, quand la chance les favorise, deviennent bien vite insupportables' (J, 47). He also establishes the role of obsession by observing that 'La force et l'endurance des rêveurs sont parfois comparables à celles des aliénés' (130). But his control is perhaps most delicately exercised through the numerous, highly inventive comic images, usually brief and pointed, which describe human and natural phenomena in unexpected terms. There are well over a

hundred of them in all, with *Manon des sources* containing
about twice as many as *Jean de Florette*. As we have seen,
Pagnol uses them to merge his characters into the landscape
and to personify nature's changing moods. But many are
designed primarily to amuse. Sometimes they are graphic but
cruel: Papet's hair is white but 'de noires pattes d'araignées
sortaient de ses narines', and Adélie has 'un grain de beauté
orné d'une virgule de poils blonds' (J, 16; 20). They mimic
actions, like the blow on the head which 'peut vous retourner le
cerveau comme une crêpe', or Jean's Asian pumpkins which
'poussent aussi vite qu'un serpent sort du trou' (55; 147). They
create pictorial impressions: a peasant drinks from the bottle
'comme une trompette'; a moon shines 'comme un œil crevé'.
Ugolin's facial contortions are described with comic hyperbole:
'une demi-douzaine de grimaces défilaient...'; ... 'tourna un
orage de tics vers le Papet...' (J, 280; M, 214-15). During the
public meeting, we see him adopt 'la mine du chasseur qui
attend le lapin à la sortie du trou', and we learn that a baby is
born 'comme une lettre à la poste, mais en sens contraire
évidemment' (M, 174; 306).

Pagnol's images usually come singly, but there are numerous
extended metaphors too, such as Papet's insistence that the
Soubeyran spark is not extinguished and will flame again, or
the religious vocabulary with which Ugolin's 'magic ceremony'
is described (M, 68; 91). The *curé*'s sermon is particularly rich in
homely, highly visual and telling images. The orphan's prayer
flies up to heaven 'comme une alouette', but Adolphin's will
never rise about his self-interest 'parce que ça n'a pas plus
d'ailes qu'un dindon plumé' (M, 194). The Bastidiens pay water
rates for the pipes which connect the spring to the fountain, but
the water is God's and must be paid for with good works: 'Vous
devez avoir une assez grosse facture en retard, et c'est pour
cela que l'administration céleste vous a fermé le robinet' (203).
The dear departed may be 'en Paradis, en train de fumer des
nuages dans une pipe de diamant', and anyone who misses an
opportunity of doing good is 'un pauvre fada qui a manqué le
train' (202).

The force of the sermon delivered by the *curé* gains
immeasurably from these extravagant images, which are not
only vivid but rooted in bluff common sense. Although Pagnol

may at times seem to abuse his narratorial authority by turning such unexpected comparisons into unfair comment on individuals unable to defend themselves (by mocking naïvety, ignorance or some physical defect, for instance), even his most barbed comments contain more affection, wisdom and moral sense than contempt. The *curé* may pepper his address with homespun images which provoke laughter quite inappropriate to the context, but he is clearly not presented in a foolish light. His story about Adolphin—whose name is inventively used as an adjective (194)—plus his reminder of the fate of the 'étranger' whose house collapsed and his talk of plucked turkeys and the Celestial Water Board, are all part of his technique of persuasion. The *curé* has his way with his flock as Pagnol has his way with his reader. Far from intending him any slight, Pagnol puts a comic masterpiece into his mouth.

Pagnol's only novel bears the stamp of technical skills built up during nearly forty years of storytelling in theatre and cinema, and it makes the most of his strengths: his ability to write convincing dialogue, his dramatist's sense of character, and his film maker's skill in constructing plot and devising absorbing, highly visual action. But it was above all through his love of language that he was able to move so effortlessly between farce and tragedy. *L'Eau des collines* deals with broken hopes and irredeemable misfortunes, yet Pagnol's control of his material, operating principally through his tone of voice which he alters at will, enables him to manipulate our reactions with absolute confidence. By varying his style, he ranges freely between irony and indulgence, but never loses faith either with the characters he creates or with his reader, whom he seeks to entertain and, when he can, instruct. He confides in us but he also teases, and his unquenchable good humour and very good jokes give colour and depth to a collection of uncensorious moral attitudes. Carefully constructed and brilliantly written, *L'Eau des collines* presents a comic view of the human condition without ever seeking to minimise the shadows which fall upon human happiness.

Chapter Seven

The Film of the Book

Pagnol's novel began as a film, and it was to the cinema that it returned in triumph in 1986. Claude Berri's thoughtful and handsome screen versions of *Jean de Florette* and *Manon des sources* proved more popular with French audiences than the other great successes of that year, *Rambo* and *Raiders of the Lost Ark*, while both parts enjoyed an uninterrupted two-year run in London, despite traditional British resistance to subtitled pictures. At the 1987 César awards, Daniel Auteuil was named Best Actor for his role as Ugolin, while in London in 1988, *Jean de Florette* received a dozen nominations and was chosen as Best Film, and *Manon des sources* was judged Best Foreign Film. When both titles were released on video they broke records everywhere for the sales of a foreign-language film. French cinema has always been admired abroad, but not even the great classics of French cinema have had such a mass appeal.

The films took seven years to plan, eight months to shoot, and consumed a budget of 110 million francs, a high figure by French standards. In 1952, Pagnol had filmed in and around the village of La Treille, which he had known since childhood. In the intervening years, urban sprawl had changed the Pagnol country beyond recognition, and summer fires had despoiled the hills. Berri was forced to look for new locations. The principal village scenes were shot at Mirabeau, twenty miles north-east of Aix-en-Provence, while the hills overlooking Cuges-les-Pins, ten miles east of Aubagne, provided natural settings which are as beautiful and as treacherous as the text requires. Other locations were Ansouis and Vaugines, and the market-place at Sommières was dressed to look as it had in 1925. Telephone wires and electric cables were buried, new buildings were masked, and 12,000 carnations were transplanted. The result was a meticulous and lovingly photographed evocation of twenties' Provence against which a strong cast played out Pagnol's seesawing saga of innocence, greed and retribution.

The screenplay (by Claude Berri and Gérard Brach) is remarkably faithful to the overall shape of Pagnol's tale. The emphasis shifts appropriately from Ugolin to Jean to Manon to Ugolin, and finally to Papet. *Jean de Florette is* a particularly efficient piece of cinema narrative. Dispensing with Pagnol's documentary preliminaries, Berri moves events forward briskly to the point where Jean Cadoret arrives at Les Romarins. Thereafter the passage of time is carefully indicated by the changing seasons and Jean's downfall is signalled by three dramatically marked betrayals (the episode of the necklace, the storm which passes him by and the sirocco) which occur in rapid succession. Jean's obsession is neatly relaunched, and his death seems entirely consistent with the mood and direction of events. In comparison, the dramatic line seems on occasion blurred in *Manon des sources*, which is stronger on minor incident and richer in secondary characters. It is less carefully paced, and the strains of adapting this more crowded second volume sometimes show. Very noticeable is the sudden, unexplained appearance of Monsieur Victor at Manon's wedding. More seriously, Manon's story is allowed to fade discreetly, so that the sense of the unstoppable continuity of things is lost.

Berri's pruning of both texts is generally sympathetic. If he cuts certain incidents (Ugolin's anti-burglar routine, for instance) and telescopes others, the effect is generally to carry the tale forward more rhythmically. Some omissions are less fortunate, however. For example, by not informing us of the manner in which Pique- Bouffigue despatched Siméon, Berri puts Papet in a much more brutal light than Pagnol intended. Giuseppe is given a walk- on part before disappearing inexplicably, and as a character, Baptistine is kept firmly in the background. Shorn of her *jettatura*, the situation loses an important element of its non- human dimension. In much the same way, the absence of Magali and the decision to allow Aimée to return to her singing career both deprive the films of a warmer tone against which certain events were judged in the books, where the women tend to have rather more common sense than the men. The result is that the burden of femininity is laid squarely on Manon, who is treated more patronizingly in the film than in the book: certain glimpses of her (playing the harmonica over Jean's grave, the embrace against the skyline) are even banal in cinema terms. Indeed, for all the sumptuous camera-work, both films are stylistically unadventurous: very rarely does Berri add touches of visual narrative (for example, the not very effective superimposition of Ugolin's vision of a field of carnations).

But Berri handles moments big and small with considerable skill. The switch from brilliantly-lit dramatic landscapes to the claustrophobic, dark dinner-table over which Papet plots so villainously, is extremely effective, while Papet's final confrontation with his fate (in the guise of blind Delphine) is magically captured in a sequence of extreme close-ups where a flicker of an eyelid and a catch in the voice reveal the full irony of fate. Moreover, there are performances to match. Yves Montand as Papet projects not only the guile of the character but also his ultimate vulnerability. Daniel Auteuil (Ugolin) manages to be both repulsive and sympathetic, while Gérard Depardieu brings out the reasonable but always deranged optimism of Jean Cadoret. And they all speak Pagnol's dialogue, which is extensively and sensitively exploited. Both films, moreover, are full of sights and sounds which more than make up for the loss of Pagnol's natural history lessons.

Despite minor reservations that are of interest only to the practised eye of close readers, Berri is faithful to the letter, simplifying without losing anything of the original rhythm or line, and also to the spirit of the novel:

> Pagnol a certes tourné sa *Manon* en 1952, Mais il devait lui rester comme une insatisfaction. Celle de n'avoir pas réellement trouvé les prolongements tragiques de sa fable. C'est pourquoi, dix ans plus tard, il l'a reprise en prose, revenant en arrière, la faisant précéder de l'histoire du père de Manon, Jean de Florette. En somme, il a donné un aboutissement littéraire à son film. Et moi, je tente aujourd'hui l'inverse. (*L'Express*, 3 janvier 1986)

Berri's recognition of the tragic dimension to Pagnol's tale is clearly signalled by his decision to underscore both films with motifs from Verdi's *The Force of Destiny*. Yves Montand was equally clear about where the emphasis lay: 'C'est une tragédie au plein sens du terme' (Le Nouvel Observateur, 22-28 septembre 1986). In certain respects, however, the films may be thought to stress the dramatic and the tragic at the expense of the comic. If this is so, it is certainly because Pagnol—inevitably—loses his narrator's voice which, as we have seen, directs our responses and constantly lightens the mood, not only with touches of humour, but obliquely, through the lavish use of ironic, deflating polysyllables.

The story of Jean's death, Ugolin's fate, Manon's revenge and Papet's tragedy provides a rare opportunity of observing how the same material may be presented in three quite different ways. Manon des sources (1952) focused attention on Manon and approached the situation from a more overtly comic point of view. It is fast-moving, very talkative, full of incident, and has a large cast of amusing secondary characters. L'Eau des collines switches the emphasis away from Manon and explores the effects of obsession in a wider range of characters, deepening their psychology and introducing, against a background of comic events and ironic comment, a new depth of tragic reverberation. The pace is slower, and the change of medium allowed Pagnol much more subtle ways of controlling the responses of his audience. Claude Berri's films, more relaxed in style than Pagnol's, are able to darken the mood further, give the story more air, and exploit silence in a way Pagnol as a film-maker never thought worth doing. Of course, by removing the layer of literary artifice which Pagnol added in his novel, Berri loses the unity of the authorial voice and a certain redeeming feyness of tone. But he gains far more, for he brings out with even greater clarity those 'prolongements tragiques' which Pagnol had himself sought. Few novels have ever been quite so accurately and elegantly transcribed for the cinema.

Conclusion

L'Eau des collines is an unashamedly old-fashioned book. Even its stoutest defenders would find it difficult to deny that its literary technique, subject and themes reflect little of the cultural, intellectual and social changes of the twentieth century.

Pagnol's omniscient narrative stance and aggressive manipulation of the reader are, by current standards, outmoded. Postwar novelists in France have preferred to work in more subtle and elusive registers, placing themselves within some philosophical or aesthetic frame of reference approved by the Parisian intelligentsia, and consciously distancing themselves from traditional realism, the 'rounded character' and the 'well-made story'. *L'Eau des collines* positively revels in unabashed storytelling, and makes no attempt to disguise its regional origins, which Pagnol exploits not only for comic purposes but also for the impact generated by the urban reader's nostalgia for the myth of country living. His novel is a kind of guided excursion which serves up enough exotic flora and fauna to satisfy the city dweller's appetite for natural history, and it comes complete with a cast of simple-minded rustics whose folkloric antics pander to our sense of superiority. It is also a highly moral, if not moralistic, fable which has the courage of its prejudices. It judges and disapproves, and requires all concerned to shoulder their own responsibilities—though, equally unfashionably, it also recognises that there are human problems which lie beyond the power of money or technology. To talk of capricious fate in our rational age which has answers for everything scarcely seems a modern stance to adopt.

Politically, it is clear that *L'Eau des collines* expresses a right-wing view of society—for all the mockery, it supports institutions like the Church and the republican order symbolised by Philoxène's office—and of personal relationships. The narrow chauvinism of the Bastidiens makes them inward-looking and mistrustful of outsiders, while their internal social structures centre upon tradition, the family and private property, an unholy alliance which fosters a spirit of

relentless and selfish materialism. Yet it is precisely to the
survival of these values that the dénouement leads: the
Soubeyran line will continue, the 'trésor' acquires a new
master and the socio-moral order is restored. Furthermore,
Pagnol defends a certain idea of class. The unquestioned
hierarchy of the village is based on age and experience and on
the wealth which both have a tendency to generate. The *curé*
and the mayor might give a spiritual and temporal lead, but
Papet's Soubeyran connections and personal astuteness earn
him a respect which makes him first among elders in what is a
small pond. Beyond the village boundaries, however, lies the
wider modern world to which Jean, Aimée, Manon and
Bernard all belong as members of the respectable lower middle
class, and Pagnol clearly has a fondness for their accentless
speech and their education. Les Bastides Blanches is a
traditional community based on economic individualism and
blatantly patriarchal authority, and the author seems content
to have it so. In literary, moral, intellectual and political terms,
then, *L'Eau des collines* seems out of step with the temper of
the postwar era. The universe it recreates so exactly has long
since been swept away by motorcars, television and tourism,
which have made our world if not a better, then at least a
smaller place.

   Yet these strictures—which apply equally to Pagnol's plays
and films—are more a worry to literary critics than they are to
the reading public, which is much less influenced by intellectual
fashions and fads. A million Pagnol titles are sold each year. In
1986, the list was headed by the first three volumes of the
Souvenirs d'enfance, followed by *Topaze*, *Marius*, and *Le
Temps des amours*, with *L'Eau des collines* in seventh position.
Though less enthusiastically received, *La Gloire de mon père*
and *Le Château de ma mère*, the meticulous screen versions of
the autobiographical *Souvenirs* made by Yves Robert and
released in 1990, further enhanced Pagnol's reputation and
brought new readers to his books. In the time that has elapsed
since his death in 1974, Pagnol has more than regained the
ground he lost during the 1950s.

   It may be that he has benefited from changes in the political
climate, which has seen left-wing ideology retreat before the
advance of modified forms of social democracy and the New

Right. The ecology movement has stimulated an interest in country matters, and though Pagnol was no more 'green' than Jean, he at least raises the issue of the 'vanishing peasantry' and the threatened rural community. He is also suspicious of technology. His remark, in his screen *Manon*, that engineers are dangerous people—'ça commence par la machine à coudre, ça finit par la bombe atomique'—strikes a curiously modern note in our disaster-conscious times. In literary terms, he has been helped by the retreat of the cerebral *nouveau roman* and by the popular vogue for the 'family saga': in this sense, *L'Eau des collines* is a hillbilly version of *Dynasty*, a kind of garlic-flavoured *Archers*. Pagnol's slow-paced, 'timeless' world no longer exists, and indeed may never have existed outside his memory of a lost Eden. Overtaken by progress, it now seems quaint and picturesque, a glimpse of the Third World located close to home. Yet paradoxically, part of the attraction lies precisely in his evocation of a lost world of simplicity and innocence, as makers of television commercials know: it is significant that Berri's films have the same kind of feel and look as a Hovis advert.

But cultural changes which have given a privileged status to nostalgia and individualism do not really account for Pagnol's enduring popularity. He was never particularly concerned with general social or moral issues and was much more a people-watcher, endowed with the imaginative capacity to span the whole of human experience from minor eccentricity to great pathos via those obsessions which may lead to happiness or to death. *L'Eau des collines* is, more than a family saga, a book of wisdom with a ready appeal: it does not tell us how to behave or think, but reminds us of how we should feel. This does not mean that Pagnol was sentimental, for his shrewd humour counters any hint of mawkishness. But he takes us back to essentials. People cannot survive without dignity any more than Les Bastides Blanches can survive without water, and dignity is a form of self-respect which must be earned. Rewards, however, may not always be granted, even to those who are more innocent than guilty: life and human happiness are precarious and constantly under threat. Pagnol, then, never content simply to amuse, was a clear-eyed moralist who did not attempt to hide the sadness which lies in wait for us all.

But if Pagnol talks to us like a kindly uncle, he speaks with the voice of a subtle and sophisticated literary artist. L'Eau des collines is seamlessly constructed and its internal symmetries create the sense of inevitability which ultimately gives the dénouement its tragic power. But it is also the novel of a film maker. It is a very visual book and certain moments—the 'charmante expédition' which brings Jean's family to Les Romarins, Manon dancing in the mountain stream or running in the moonlight—are pure cinema. But Pagnol is also a master of moods, and he mixes documentary realism with a mysterious sense of poetry which lifts off into airy regions where elemental truths are most clearly visible. His manipulation of the reader, whose status as 'superior' observer is at crucial moments removed, is likewise calculated to make us feel the full force of the drama into which we are plunged when we are least expecting it. Pagnol's total control of his material is matched only by his command of language. He is at home in every register: he mimics 'le parler Provençal', parodies 'le beau style', descends into vulgarity and commits himself to flights of fancy. The curé's sermon, with its richly comic images and resonant phrasing, is a masterpiece of eloquence. Pagnol's descriptive prose is rhythmical, exact and graphic and, perhaps most stunning of all, the dialogue sparkles brilliantly, filling out character, maintaining the drama at a high level and keeping us constantly amused. It is the measure of his artistry that he succeeds in giving the grim theme of fate a comic treatment without ever compromising the gravity of his subject. He does not make light of human misery, but neither does he lose his sense of proportion. Maintaining this delicate balance between humour and seriousness is perhaps the most difficult of the technical miracles which Pagnol triumphantly resolves.

Throughout his career Marcel Pagnol was never taken seriously by the literary establishment, which regarded him as a popular entertainer in the middlebrow range. His sins in their eyes were few but large. Firstly, he never expressed a cogent philosophy, nor was he interested in arguments about art and ideas. Secondly, he was a comic writer with a line in homespun truth. Thirdly, he was highly successful. Pagnol was not entirely immune to such hostile criticisms but he consoled himself with the view that, in literary matters, final verdicts are always delivered by the paying public. His popular image has grown considerably since his death in 1974, and currently his star waxes very bright indeed. He continues to delight and disarm new generations of readers and cinemagoers, as once he did their parents and grandparents. The Prousts and the Sartres are admired. But Pagnol, who has become a national institution, has managed rather more: he is regarded, quite simply, with affection.

Glossary

Provençal, Semi-Provençal and Regional Words

The scholarly assistance of Dr. Peter V. Davies is gratefully acknowledged. Provençal words are given in italics.

agachon (*agachoun*), n.m. — a hide; 'sorte de cabane de verdure' (J, 163)

alude (*aludo*), n.f. — large flying ant

argéras (*argelas*), n.m. — gorse

baouco (*bauco*), n.m. — tough, coarse grass

bastide (*bastido*), n.f. — country or farm house

bourscarle (*bouscarlo*), n.f. — warbler

bousquetier (cf. *busquejaire*), n.m — wood-cutter

cabridan (cf. *cabrian*), n.m. — hornet

cade (*cade*), n.m. — large juniper

cagagne (*cagagno*), n.f. — gripes, diarrhoea

caganis (*cagonis*, last-born), n.m. — term of affection

ciste (cf. *ciste*), n.m. — Stinking Hellebore 'que les Anglais appellent 'la rose des roches' et les Provençaux la 'messugue' (M, 286)

coucourde (*coucourdo*), n.f. — pumpkin

cul-blanc (*cuou-blanc*), n.m. — whitear

ensuquer (*ensuca*) — to stun

escagasser (*escagassa*) — to crush, shatter

s'escagasser — to be overwhelmed, dumbfounded; collapse

esculette (*esqueleto*, n.f.), n.m. — skeleton

espaloufier (cf. *espala*) — to overwhelm

espigaou (cf. *espigado*, n.f.), n.m. — ear, head of grain; spike of flower

s'estransiner (*s'estransina*) — to be overcome (by emotion)

estrasses (*estrasserié*), n.f. — old rags; tatters

fada (*fadas*) — simple-minded; simpleton

garrigue (*garrigo*, from pre-Latin 'garric', oak), n.f. — moorland

graffigner, graffignure (*grafigna, grafignage*, n.m.) — to scratch; a scratch

gratte-cul (='églantier'), n.m. — dog-rose, briar

larmeuse (*lagramuso*), n.f. — small lizard
lentisque (*lentiscle*), n.m. — mastic-tree
limbert (*limbert*), n.m. — green lizard
loube (*loubo* = teeth of she-wolf), n.f. — saw

machote (*machoto*), n.f. — short-eared owl
mas (*mas*), n.m. — farm or country house
messugue, n.f. — see *ciste*
migon (*migoun*), n.m. — sheep droppings

parpeléger (*parpeleja*) — to blink, twitch
pèbre d'ail (*pebre d'ai*—poivre d'ail, or ... *d'ase*— ... d'âne), n.m. — savory
pétélin (*petelin*), n.m. — terebinth, turpentine tree
picosse (cf. *picosso*), n.f. — wood-axe
pigne (*pigno*), n.f. — pine cone
planette (*planet*, n.m.), n.f. — small plateau
polenta, n.f. — Italian dish of porridge made from barley meal

pourridié (*pourridié*), n.m. — rotting matter
pregadiou (*prègo-Diéu*), n.m. — praying mantis

ratepénade (*rato-penado*, n.f.), n.m. — bat
redorto (P.*redorto*, n.f.), n.m. — clematis
rouste (*roustìo*), n.f. — volley of blows

serpolet (cf. *serpoul*), n.m. — variety of thyme

térébinthe, n.m. — see *pétélin*

vin de jacquez, n.m. — 'Le vin noir des collines natales' (J, 303), from an American variety immune to the phylloxera disease.

Bibliography

References in the text are to the 1988 Fortunio edition of *L'Eau des collines* (orig. publ. 1963). The work has been translated into English by W.E. van Heyningen, and is available as *The Water of the Hills: Jean de Florette and Manon of the Springs*, in hardback (André Deutsch, 1962) and paperback (Pan: Picador Books, 1988). Pagnol's early work for the theatre is discussed in some detail in my edition of *Topaze* (Harrap, 1981).

Most of Pagnol's writings have been issued under a variety of imprints, the most recent of which are Presses Pocket and, currently, the Éditions de Fallois. Readers wishing to examine *Judas* for themselves, however, will have to consult the twelve-volume *Œuvres complètes* published by 'Le Club de l'Honnête Homme' (1970-71).

Among critical studies, the following will be found useful:

Aubarède, Gabriel d'   'Un débutant nommé Pagnol', in *Les Nouvelles Littéraires*, no. 1863, 16 mai 1963.

Berni, Georges   *Merveilleux Pagnol*. Monte-Carlo, Éditions Pastorelly, 1981.

Beylie, Claude   *Marcel Pagnol*. Paris, Seghers, 'Cinéma d'aujourd'hui, 80', 1974.

Caldicott, C.E.J.   *Marcel Pagnol*. Boston, Twayne, 'Twayne's World Author Series, 391', 1977.

Castans, Raymond   *Marcel Pagnol m'a raconté...* Paris, Éd. de Provence / Éd. de la Table Ronde, 1975.

——————————   *Marcel Pagnol: biographie*. Paris, Lattès, 1987.

Coward, David

Pagnol: *'La Gloire de mon père'* and *'Le Château de ma mère'*. London: Grant & Cutler, 'Critical Guides to French Texts, 96', 1992.

Georges, Yvonne S.

Les Provençalismes de 'L'Eau des collines', roman de Marcel Pagnol: étude de langue. Aix-en-Provence, Publications des Annales de la Faculté de lettres (Série: Travaux et Mémoires, 42), 1987 [first published 1966].

Klotz, Roger

'Le vocabulaire et le style de Pagnol dans *Jean de Florette'*, in *Marseille*, no. 150 (1988), pp. 54-7.

Rat, Maurice

'Succulence des romans de Marcel Pagnol', in *Vie et Langage* (mars 1964), pp. 147-50.

Filmography

MANON DES SOURCES (1952)

Prod. Les Films Marcel Pagnol. Written and directed by Marcel Pagnol. Camera: Willy Factorovitch. Music: Raymond Legrand.

With: Jacqueline Bouvier (Manon), Rellys (Ugolin), Raymond Pellegrin (Maurice), Annie Roudier (his mother), Robert Vattier (Monsieur Belloiseau), René Sarvil (the police sergeant), Henri Poupon (Le Papet), Blavette (Pamphile), Milly Mathis (Amélie), Henri Vilbert (the *curé*), Fernand Sardou (Philoxène), Delmont (Anglade), Jean Panisse (Éliacin), Edmond Ardisson (Ange), Arius (Claudius).

Running time: 190 mins.

JEAN DE FLORETTE (1986)

Prod. Renn-Productions / Antenne 2 TV France / Films A2 / RAI TV2 / Télévision Suisse Romande / DD Productions. Adaptation by Claude Berri and Gérard Brach. Director: Claude Berri. Camera: Bruno Nuytten. Set Design: Bernard Vezat. Music: Jean-Claude Petit, with the Orchestre de Paris. *Jean de Florette* harmonica theme, played by Toots Thielemans, from *The Force of Destiny,* by Verdi.

With: Yves Montand (Le Papet), Gérard Depardieu (Jean), Daniel Auteuil (Ugolin), Aimée (Élisabeth Depardieu), Ernestine Mazurowna (young Manon), Margarita Lozano (Baptistine), Amandine (Chantal Liennel), Philoxène (Armand Meffre), Pamphile (André Dupon), Casimir (Pierre Nougaro), Pascal (Pierre-Jean Rippert), Martial (Marc Betton), Anglade (Jean Maurel), Ange (Roger Souza), Éliacin (Didier Pain), Pique-Bouffigue (Marcel Champel), Giuseppe (Benedetto Bertino), Médéric (Clément Cal).

Running Time: 114 mins.

MANON DES SOURCES (1986)

Production credits as for *Jean de Florette*.

With: Yves Montand (Le Papet), Daniel Auteuil (Ugolin), Manon (Emmanuelle Béart), Hippolyte Girardot (Bernard), Aimée (Élisabeth Depardieu), Margarita Lozano (Baptistine), Philoxène (Armand Meffre), Pamphile (André Dupon), Cabridan (Pierre-Jean Rippert), Martial (Marc Betton), Casimir (Pierre Nougaro), Anglade (Jean Maurel), Ange (Roger Souza), Éliacin (Didier Pain), Yvonne Gamay (Delphine), Lucien Damiani (Monsieur Belloiseau), Jean Bouchard (the *curé*), Tiki Olgado (the *spécialiste*).

Running Time: 122 mins.

Jean de Florette and *Manon des sources* were made available on video in France by Proserpine (1987). British video release: February 1989, on Palace Video, PVC 4045A and 4046A, both with PG certificate.